BEYOND THE POWER STRUGGLE

BEYOND
the
POWER STRUGGLE
A Guide for Parents of Challenging Kids

Richard Selznick, Ph.D.

SENTIENT PUBLICATIONS

First Sentient Publications edition 2023
Copyright © 2023 by Richard Selznick, PhD

A paperback original

Cover design by Kim Johansen, Black Dog Design
Book design by Timm Bryson, em em design, llc

Publisher's Cataloging-in-Publication data

Names: Selznick, Richard, author.
Title: Beyond the power struggle : a guide for parents of challenging kids / Richard Selznick, Ph.D
Description: Boulder, CO : Sentient Publications, 2023.
Identifiers: LCCN: 2023041068 | ISBN: 978-1-59181-310-1
Subjects: LCSH Child rearing. | Parenting. | Behavior disorders in children. | Attention-deficit hyperactivity disorder. | BISAC FAMILY & RELATIONSHIPS / Parenting / General | FAMILY & RELATIONSHIPS / Life Stages / School Age | FAMILY & RELATIONSHIPS / Conflict Resolution | FAMILY & RELATIONSHIPS / Attention Deficit Disorder (ADD-ADHD)
Classification: LCC HQ773 .S45 2023 | DDC 649/.64—dc23

Printed in the United States of America

10 9 8 7 6 5 4 3 2 1

SENTIENT PUBLICATIONS
A Limited Liability Company
PO Box 1851
Boulder, CO 80306
www.sentientpublications.com

Contents

Contents

To my friend and long-term colleague,
Pamela Goldberger. Thank you for years of support,
advice, friendship, and encouragement.
I could not have done it without you.

Preface

Before diving into the principles of this book, I want to lay out a few points.

As a psychologist who has logged in a fair amount of mileage working with children and parents, I don't pretend to have all the answers.

I recognize that in this business, much depends on whose doorstep you land. That is, if you go to a neurologist, you may get one view, a psychiatrist, psychologist, or behaviorist, three others. Every psychologist who works with children may use totally different approaches and methods.

Some will emphasize behavioral approaches. Others may insist on individual child therapy where the parents have minimal direct involvement in the process. Some may be applying more "CBT" (Cognitive-Behavior-Therapy) methods, while others are applying family systems theories.

Much depends on the professional's orientation and their level of training, along with their own professional experiences and where they went for further continuing education.

For me, I cut my teeth fairly early on in my career at the Philadelphia Child Guidance Clinic where some of the pioneers of family therapy had developed their theories. I enjoyed the experience, and, in many ways, it never left me.

I was also influenced by supervisors and mentors who subscribed to a type of individual child therapy model that was grounded in Freudian thinking that now seems like ancient voodoo. I still remember having the child play or draw pictures which were then symbolically interpreted.

Above all, I have the influence of my father, Mel Selznick, firmly planted in my psyche. To this day, I have never seen anyone who had a greater gift for making a child feel better about himself or herself. As a principal, teen-worker, camp director, and athletic director my dad was a champion of the underdog.

In my own way, I'd like to believe I have kept up the family tradition. It still warms me when I see a kid walk out of the office with a slightly lighter step than when they came in.

A Disclaimer

Apropos of some of my points above, what I am offering is my perspective, my opinion.

The subject of parenting can be as controversial as the political landscape; people can tie themselves in knots over a perspective or view that they disagree with. I have no claims on the truth. I have interacted with thousands of children and their parents and heard their stories. That's what underlies much of what's being said here.

It is impossible to generalize. It's always child by child, family by family. Each one is unique for countless variables. With that said, there will be principles shared with you that I think can be helpful as you try to manage your challenging child.

My overriding mission as expressed in my previous books and through my website www.shutdownlearner.com, with over 550 blog posts at the time of this writing, is to talk to parents in down-to-earth, plain language, with as little jargon or terminology as possible, like we were having a living room chat.

Hopefully, I've accomplished that mission with this text. Come into the living room and enjoy. Stay a while.

Introduction

Are you overwhelmed and challenged by your child's behavior?

Do you find yourself reluctant at times to take your child to public places like restaurants or birthday parties?

Does your child have meltdowns in playgroups or grab other kids' toys? Do you worry that the other parents may be talking about how your child is "out of control?"

If the answer to any of these questions or others like them is "yes," then this parenting guidebook may help you.

While every child is unique and complex in their own way, some are more challenging and difficult for parents to manage than others. Working with these children and families has given rise to perhaps my number one truism: "Challenging children are challenging."

Challenging kids are those who, when they encounter the slightest bit of frustration or difficulty, become highly reactive and demanding, often going into fits of rage. Once these children are triggered, they commonly scream, cry, or run around the house in outrage. They frequently hit parents and siblings or even break things.

Their parents then become frazzled, overwhelmed, and exhausted, and tensions within the family escalate. A cycle develops that is almost impossible to break.

My role is to provide guidance to parents to help break that cycle.

In my years as a child psychologist, much of my practice has focused on children's behavioral issues. By necessity, this involves supporting and advising parents, who feel helpless in the face of their child's struggle to cope with even the most ordinary situations and expectations.

Shifting Your Parenting Mindset

By way of introduction, I consider myself to be a bit of a "salmon-swimmer"—that is, I frequently see myself going against the current, often reluctant to use popular psychological theories or neurobiological explanations for a child's behavior.

I'm also keenly aware that a parent who consults five different professionals is likely to receive five different opinions and recommended courses of action, each involving varying amounts of time and money and a different set of interventions.

A parent of a challenging child is usually faced with trending parenting topics, opinions from friends and family members, and an abundance of misinformation about children's behavior on social media—and this gives them a bewildering range of options for dealing with a child's behavior.

The overall goal of this book is to shift your parenting mindset and style. As you come to understand your child's basic temperament, you will modify your manner, style, and attitude in interacting with the child, and this will impact their behavior.

Over the years, I have seen how a shift in the parent's mindset and attitude can lead to moderate to considerable behavioral changes in the child. These changes will be additive and incremental. Over time they will lead to significant growth for your child, which will greatly reduce tension in the family.

For example, Cecelia, the mom of two children ages four and six, was having a terrible time taking them to any store or restaurant (even child-friendly ones). I suggested she make a couple of small changes, and within a week or two, Cecelia was ecstatic about the changes she observed with her children.

While this is not a "how-to" parenting book in the classic sense, there will be specific suggestions that you can implement and practice right away.

These suggestions will likely be effective—regardless of whether your child has an identified neurobiological disorder such as ADHD or whether their behavior is driven by innate temperament (and perhaps a few parenting missteps).

Reading this book may, at times, feel a bit unsettling; in fact, some of your strongly held parenting beliefs or philosophies may be challenged. Examining your underlying attitudes, which is what we're doing here, is rarely an easy task.

But it is certainly a worthwhile one.

THE NATURE OF CHALLENGING CHILDREN

Same As It Ever Was

We live in a decaying age. Young people no longer respect their parents. They are rude and impatient. They frequently inhabit places they shouldn't and have no self-control.

—Inscription found in a
6,000-year-old Egyptian tomb

When I was young, we were taught to be discreet and respectful of elders, but the present youth are exceedingly disrespectful and impatient of restraint.

—Hesiod, 8th Century BCE

Our youth now love luxury. They have bad manners, contempt for authority; they show disrespect for their elders and love chatter in place of exercise; they no longer rise when elders enter the room; they contradict their parents; chatter before company; gobble up their food and tyrannize their teachers.

—Socrates, 469 BCE

The world is passing through troubled times. The young people of today think of nothing but themselves. They have no reverence for parents or old age. They are impatient of all restraint. They talk as if they knew everything, and what passes for wisdom with us is foolishness with them. As for the girls, they are forward, immodest, and unladylike in speech, behavior, and dress.

—From a sermon preached by
Peter the Hermit in 1274

Children are natural mimics—they act like their parents in spite of every attempt to teach them good manners.

—Mad Magazine

Or as the Talking Heads said in their classic song "Once in a Lifetime"— "Same as it ever was. Same as it ever was."

Apparently, the idea that the world is going to hell in a handbasket is nothing new. For at least six thousand years, adults have commented on humanity's downward spiral as embodied by the younger generation.

My guess is that most of us are at least a little guilty of this. We shake our heads and wonder, *What's the matter with kids these days?* Or we ask the next logical question: *What's the matter with modern parents? Why are they so indulgent with their difficult* [or they may think bratty] *children?*

It's easy to lose perspective. For example, many parents complain and worry about their child's overuse of screens. This anxiety can be pervasive.

But what if I told these parents that I could absolutely guarantee that their children would stop spending so much time on their screens, but that there would be one catch? The catch would be that the parents would also have to turn off their cell phones (and Apple watches) when they weren't being used for work.

This would take care of the kids' screen time problems—but how many parents would raise their hands and sign up to do their part?

I have posed that same question to large workshops full of parents. And I have never seen a single hand raised.

We all make our compromises.

That being said, let's start exploring the role of a child's temperament, which often sets the tone for how their childhood will look.

Temperament Style and the Bell Curve

A basic premise of this book is that a child's temperament style is the primary variable influencing their behavior. Let's think for a moment about the classic bell curve.

For most traits that can be measured, such as anxiety, sociability, or self-confidence, if we plot a few hundred children on a graph, most will fall into the middle, average range for these traits. That is, relatively few kids will be extremely self-confident, for instance, or extremely unsociable.

Statistically, we know that about 70% of those measured would fall within the average range in the middle part of the curve. Only about 15% would be on the far-right or the far-left part of the curve.

When it comes to challenging children, the bell curve helps us to see that they are outliers. Their behavior, in terms of coping, managing frustration, interacting with friends, managing expectations, or behaving in general, is outside the average range on the curve.

Unlike some psychologists who think that children struggle to cope or behave as a direct result of parenting, I see it as primarily a result of their temperament. In other words, temperamentally speaking, each child is wired in a particular way: easy or difficult, flexible or inflexible. It's largely the child's "makeup," or their personality style, that determines their characteristic mode or style of interacting.

Or in other words, once again—challenging children are challenging. And temperament is on a spectrum from mild to challenging in nature.

I'm not suggesting that temperamentally difficult children may not also have a disability or a neurological disorder such as ADHD. But challenging children are often just given a neurological diagnosis without further exploration of their issues, implying that their behavior is only medically based and medical treatment alone will change it.

Looking through the lens of temperamental style, however, we usually end up reinterpreting the child's behavioral struggles. Rather than being the result of some disorder, they arise more from the child's positioning on the temperament spectrum.

This perspective of temperament does not let the parent off the hook entirely for shaping their child's behavior. It is important to remember, though, that parents are not the sole reason why a child is behaving a particular way or is difficult in general—often parents, moms more so than dads, receive unnecessary blame.

Group A

When it comes to temperament, kids can generally be divided into two groups: those who fall to the right of center (Group A) and those who fall to the left of center (Group B).

On the right side of the bell curve, Group A children tend to have a more flexible and easygoing temperament. This means they usually handle curveballs and changing expectations pretty well.

For example, you can tell them, "Sorry, we're not going to McDonald's tonight as we had originally planned," and it's not the end of the world. The child handles it. There may be a degree of disappointment, but no extreme reaction.

While these children may cry occasionally, depending upon their age, they are not prone to excessive meltdowns or tantrums. Typically social and popular, they are readily invited over to other children's houses for play dates and other activities. Further, when faced with challenges or difficulties, they do not tend to give up easily.

In terms of their day-to-day functioning, they don't require a great deal of parental input, even at a young age.

Teachers see them as a pleasure, and their interaction and behavior in the classroom are considered age-appropriate. They get many compliments and positive attention from adults.

In short, Group A children are viewed as easy. However, it is important to keep in mind that while flexibility is normally perceived as a positive trait, an extremely flexible or easy temperament can be problematic too. As these children develop, it may be difficult for them to stand up for themselves or even to identify how they truly feel or what they want.

Group B

On the left side of the curve, Group B children are a different story altogether.

While these children have their charms and are often a lot of fun, they show a predominantly inflexible style. From a young age they are characteristically prone to fits of anger at the slightest difficulty. Small limits set can lead to major reactions, such as meltdowns, fits of sobbing, and expressions of rage. ("But you promised we were going to McDonald's," the child screams, as they cry and carry on at great length.)

Overall, these children can be quite demanding in their inability to manage the ordinary requests that emerge on a daily basis. Not coping well with basic frustration or ordinary demands, these children can be quite reactive, especially when parents or teachers tell them "No."

Parents are continually challenged to manage these children.

On a nightly basis, refusal to start or finish homework can lead to an ongoing struggle. They often have difficulty following basic directions and may ignore and break established rules, leaving parents feeling quite frustrated.

From about the age of three onward, meltdowns become common whenever the child is asked to do something that they do not like doing, such as getting off their iPad, turning off a video game or starting homework. Sibling battles can prove excessive.

Since their challenging behaviors also emerge in social situations outside the home, these children are rarely invited on play dates. Their characteristic inflexibility is rarely an ingredient for social success.

Not an Either-Or Proposition

It is important to remember that these two groups represent temperamental tendencies and that they are not either-or distinctions.

Rather than view a child as definitively fitting in one category or the other, I prefer to think of them as having a dominant personality style. Based on the typical or characteristic ways they conduct themselves, both at home and in social situations, a child can be thought of as primarily a Group A or Group B.

This also means that there is no one objective test, like a COVID-19 test or an x-ray, that tells whether your child is in one group or another. It all comes down to the weight of the evidence.

When you look at the bell curve, the farther away from the midpoint the child seems to be, the more confident you can be about that child's characteristic temperamental style. Also, the farther from the midpoint the child falls, the more reason you have for thinking that this temperamental style may represent a legitimate, diagnosable disorder, such as ADHD.

This question of a disorder is considered a pressing one—parents come to my office all the time wanting to know if their child "has it." As in, "Tell it to me straight, Doc, does he have ADHD?"

My answer is "maybe, but maybe not."

There's a complex relationship between a child's temperament, their behavior, and any neurological conditions they may have. For example, a child might have a temperament that is anxious in nature, but does that mean that the child has an anxiety disorder? If the anxiety is mild to more moderate, then maybe not. If the anxiety is constant and severe, then maybe so.

Similarly, children tend to be fairly distractible by nature. To make a big generalization, boys in particular have never been known for their high-level capacity to pay attention in school. But does this mean that all boys have a brain-based disability/disorder, such as ADHD?

No, it does not. But *some* boys (and girls)—those whose distractibility is extreme—may actually have ADHD.

This mindset is different than the more typical medical/psychological explanations of a child's behavior. These explanations typically offer a firm diagnosis of "yes, he has it" or "no, he does not have it."

Some may object to this perspective, thinking that it is better to name something and give it a label. But I think that labeling tends to be associated with the mindset that the child's behavior or issues can be explained almost entirely by a label such as "ADHD."

So, I do not advocate an emphasis on labeling; rather, there are often multiple interacting factors motivating a child's behavior.

I'm not saying that a child's psychological or neurological issues should be ignored. Rather, the bell curve perspective described in this section normalizes the kind of temperamental differences and ranges that we see in the whole human population.

This perspective can help parents move away from thinking that their child's struggles must be based on some disability, which I call "disability thinking." Disability thinking can be pretty limiting for both parents and kids. The alternative view helps people develop a broader perspective, that is, normalizing rather than pathologizing.

Is Parenting at the Heart of the Problem? (Not So Fast)

In addition to the labels and diagnoses offered as explanations for a child's behavior, it is often assumed that parenting is a significant reason, if not the primary reason, for a child's behavior.

When we see a Group A child (the flexible type), we think or say how lovely the child is and how great a job the parents did in raising the child. That is, the child's behavior is viewed as a direct outgrowth of good parenting.

On the other hand, when we see a Group B child (the challenging type), we assume that bad parenting underlies the difficult behavior. Whether we say it out loud or not, we make an inherent judgment that the parent has been permissive and overly indulgent. In other words, we think the child is running the show. This mindset is ingrained in our thinking.

While parenting certainly has a big influence on how a child behaves, it's not the entire story.

With families that I have seen over the years who have more than one child, typically one child has an easier, more flexible temperament, and the other is more inflexible, rigid, and

21

demanding. If parenting were the primary influence on behavior, it would stand to reason that both siblings would be similar in their behavioral style.

I've even observed this with twins: one twin is flexible and easygoing (Group A) and the other is challenging (Group B).

My essential message is that temperament is a ruling variable that determines a child's behavior, parenting being only one component. As I mentioned earlier, that does not mean that parents are entirely off the hook—but they are not squarely to blame.

This leads to the question: If a child's temperament is at the heart of the issue, why are parents and parenting the primary focus in this text?

Here's my answer: While parents can't change their child's temperament, they can modify the way they interact with their child, which can lead to positive effects on a child's behavior. This helps change the odds for the better in any given situation.

This is why, even though parenting may not be the primary reason for the child's behavior, parenting style is still the primary focus in this book. Later on, we'll discuss what I call "matter-of-fact parenting," which is a parenting style that I've seen have great results for challenging Group B children and their families.

Summary

At the heart of this book is the notion that children fall into one of two broad temperament categories – those on the easier, more flexible side and those who are viewed as challenging, inflexible, and difficult.

For a variety of reasons, parents have a tremendously difficult time figuring out how to parent and manage these children. The issues of concern occur on a spectrum ranging from fairly mild to moderately challenging and more severe.

The more severe the problems, the greater the strain is put on the parents and the family. Eventually, the family system reaches a breaking or boiling point.

While there are no "fixes" in the traditional sense, there is a parental mindset, an attitude that can help shift things so tensions in the family can be reduced to more manageable levels. The work required to make this shift is not easy, as the ways in which we respond interpersonally to others and to stress are deeply ingrained. However, over time, we can make incremental changes and the results we see can be significant.

Contrary to popular belief, parents are not the cause of children's challenging behaviors. Despite this, parents must be the ones to implement change as children are generally not reflective or introspective enough to initiate it.

SECTION II

STORIES & VIGNETTES

In this section, I offer stories and vignettes providing some insight into the temperament of the Group B children, the dynamics underlying their behavior, and how parents interact with this temperament style. These are all taken from my actual interactions with children and parents over the years.

(A quick note before we get farther into this section: I usually speak in the singular, about "a" parent or "the" parent. However, if there's more than one parent in the mix, then whatever I'm saying applies to both of them unless specified otherwise.)

A Peek Inside a Group B Brain

Perhaps a speculative glimpse into the mind of Liam, an eleven-year-old boy who shows Group B characteristics, will offer some insight. Trying to understand what Liam is thinking to himself helps us better understand what we are dealing with.

As a general rule, Liam can be quite moody and difficult, particularly when he's asked to do anything school-related. Liam's style of coping with school presents an ongoing challenge for his parents.

On a regular weekday evening, Liam thinks to himself:

They're at it again. I just want to be left alone. Homework is stupid. I hear my mom yelling at my dad about that 504 Plan, whatever that is. I heard something like "extra time". My mom seems to want it. Why would I want extra time? I want less time. Double time! Are they kidding me? I hate this stuff.

Oh, no. They're taking me to that doctor again tomorrow. He's the one that said I've got this thing—like in my brain or something—I forget what he called it. It had some letters smooshed together, like ADD something.

School is just so boring. I mean, how many of these stupid worksheets can they hand out— "circle this; cross out that." Just because they put a picture on the top of the sheet doesn't make it fun. They think the picture will keep kids wanting to do it. It's like all the teacher knows are these stupid worksheets. Ugh. I can't stand it.

The girls really bug me. They get smiley faces all the time. They always look so happy. They are so annoying. I know the teacher likes them best. She always seems bugged by me. Last week, she told me they were going to have a meeting about me soon to talk about my 504 Plan.

I only know one other kid who I think has this 504 thing— Noah—and he is such an idiot. He always acts so stupid. Why am I getting it too?

I just want to play Fortnite—why can't I do that? I just want to be left alone to play my video games.

Seven-Year-Old Mitchell Wants What He Wants

Then there's seven-year-old Mitchell. In contrast to his five-year-old sister, Gabriella, Mitchell is oppositional, difficult, and demanding. Prone to meltdowns when he does not get his way, Mitchell has extreme reactions whenever his parents ask him to do something he does not want to do.

What does Mitchell want?

That's simple. Mitchell wants what he wants when he wants it—Mitchell wants pleasure.

For most modern kids, pleasure comes from screens and related devices, such as playing video games, engaging with an iPad, using a cell phone, or watching YouTube (or "Tubing" as they say) or TikTok.

When inflexible and difficult children are separated from their devices, they can make a parent's life miserable with their extreme behavior.

This is definitely the case with Mitchell.

Whenever he is asked to do something that is not pleasurable—like turn off the screen and do some homework or get ready for bed—Mitchell reacts very poorly, throwing himself on the ground, crying and flailing around, and screaming, "I just want to play more—I'm not tired."

At these times, Mitchell does as he pleases, running the show and holding his mother and father hostage. Mitchell's parents aren't what I'd call pushovers, but they feel overwhelmed and at a loss as to how to respond when he's in one of his states—which are quite frequent.

Not knowing how to handle him, Mitchell sends his parents into states of despair and anguish. Mitchell's mother feels overwhelmed, depleted, and exhausted, while his father is angry, frequently blaming his wife for their son's behavior.

Mitchell's father believes that his mother should be tougher on him, but Mitchell's mother knows that his father is unaware how often he also gives in to Mitchell's excessive and continual demands.

Olivia, the "Queen of Hearts"

Jennifer, the mom of a challenging and difficult nine-year-old girl named Olivia, says to me, "I guess I really messed things up, didn't I?"

Her daughter is very demanding and "meltdowny" (a word I made up but find much use for). In response to the slightest bit of frustration or difficulty, Olivia screams, cries, and flails around.

Jennifer tells the story of her attempts to pick out a communion dress for Olivia.

Every dress Jennifer picked out online was quickly dismissed by Olivia, who screamed at her mother, "I hate it! I hate it!" Olivia threw herself on the floor in spasmodic fits, while Jennifer kept scouring the internet for just the right dress.

When they try dress shopping in person at the store, Olivia behaves the same way. This public display is very embarrassing for Jennifer.

As Jennifer tells the story of the demanding Olivia, one can easily picture Olivia as the Queen of Hearts in *Alice in Wonderland*, screaming, "Off with their heads! Off with their heads!" while the playing card servants run around trying to please the queen.

Olivia is, indeed, a very demanding queen. And Jennifer's comment at the beginning of this story fits a bigger pattern.

Parents (usually the moms) will feel like they "messed up." It is their core belief that that if they were a different kind of parent, their demanding and difficult child would be more flexible and easygoing.

Jennifer feels solely responsible for Olivia's behaviors.

As indicated earlier, I do not see it that way. It is my impression that moms are all too quick to blame themselves and take it on the chin, which does not hold up under closer analysis of the variables and the realities of the situation.

William, an "Opposite Child"

Some time ago, I observed a four-year-old preschooler named William who was considered a very challenging child. I thought of William as an "opposite child" (another term I made up). In other words, he tried to do the exact opposite of what everyone else wanted him to do, whether it was within his school, peer group or family.

You probably know the phrase "going with the grain"—but that did not describe William. William was a "grain-rubber," always going against the grain.

In his preschool class, William rarely followed the rules of a game or did what the teacher asked. The other children became angry and frustrated with his grain-rubbing and wanted nothing to do with him.

At home, William cries to his mother, "No one likes me in school—they all hate me."

Even when the teacher patiently explained things to him, William never saw his role in or contribution to these negative classroom interactions. He largely thought they were all the other children's fault and that everyone was against him.

After I observed and assessed William, his parents and I did a lot of work together so that they could better manage his challenging behaviors by establishing effective limits and expectations.

But this was no easy task.

To try and have his demands met, William continually pushed parental buttons. Insisting that the family only eat food that he liked, like French fries and cheeseburgers, William went into a rage if his parents put something else on the table.

When other children came over to play, they had to play only the games that William wanted to play. William almost never compromised if the other children wanted to play something different.

Over the years, I lost touch with William and his family, but when William was a young adult, his dad came in to say hello and update me.

As a 23-year-old medical student, William had come a long way, but in the story his dad told about the adult William, there were signs of the same temperament I'd seen in the four-year-old "opposite child."

For instance, William had a way of acting like he was superior to the other medical students. He was also one of the few students who frequently challenged his professors when he considered them to be wrong.

Even in adulthood, no one viewed William as a flexible person who went with the flow. From four years of age to twenty-three, William never took the easy route.

Amelia Ignores Her Mom

Eight-year-old Amelia largely goes about her day ignoring her mom, Andrea.

Andrea's tendency is to try and get Amelia to comply, but she largely talks to her in an insecure and hesitant voice ("Now, come on Amelia, how about we start cleaning up?"). The result is that Amelia entirely tunes her out.

Unfortunately, Andrea's voice and style do not convey an expectation or belief that she thinks Amelia will comply.

To a child like Amelia, Andrea's weak attempts to get her to do what she asks are like nails on a chalkboard, and she becomes annoyed by her mother's ineffective requests. Internally sneering at her mom's weakness, Amelia dismisses and neglects her mother and any requests made. As this dance between them continues, Andrea becomes increasingly irritated, and it begins to show.

After feeling completely dismissed, ignored, and disrespected, Andrea yells in rage, "Damn it, Amelia! I asked you to clean up. I'm sick of this. Why can't you just listen the first time?"

Afraid of losing control even further, Andrea starts to angrily put away the toys while Amelia stands by idly. After some time and seeing how angry her mother is, Amelia begins a half-hearted attempt to put away one toy at a time while her mother does 98% of the work.

This enrages Andrea even more.

What makes Andrea angrier still is that while Amelia slowly puts things away, her body becomes limp in a "guava jelly-like" state of noncompliance. As she goes into this posture, it almost appears as if she lacks the musculoskeletal capacity to put the things away, even though twenty minutes ago she had scattered them all around the room.

When the evening finally draws to a close, Andrea faces another ritual that she dreads—the nightly argument between her and her husband over Amelia's behavior.

The negative feelings associated with this marital conflict then add even more fuel to her anger and frustration the next time that Amelia ignores her.

Nicholas: Anger-Fueled

If I told you that thirteen-year-old Nicholas was inconsistent in handing in his homework and that he tended to avoid responsibility, procrastinated, and seemed unable to sustain mental effort, what does that sound like to you?

Most likely you're thinking ADHD of the inattentive variety, along with "executive function deficiencies" (currently a popular term). In fact, this is exactly what Nicholas' teachers thought, and they were always making suggestions that the parents should explore it further by consulting with a psychiatrist or pediatric neurologist.

Nicholas' parents understood the teachers' unspoken implication that perhaps their son should be put on medication. But Nicholas was also a very angry child, and as I thought about his situation, a question nagged at me: What role might anger be playing in Nicholas' difficulties?

I came to think that in his case, anger was a significant variable.

As a raw emotion, anger has a way of depleting "emotional fuel" from a child's tank. As a result of the child's anger, parents frequently implement a series of reactive punishments, like no more video games until further notice or being grounded for the weekend. Eventually, the anger transforms into an underlying river of unspoken resentment within the child.

How does Nicholas react to this? Does he go off and reflect, *Gee, my parents are right—I do deserve to have my gaming system taken away, so now I'll start doing my homework more consistently?*

I doubt it.

His internal monologue was probably more like this:

This is so unfair. Their stupid punishments won't work. I can't believe they are doing this. I'll show them. I'm not going to do the stupid work no matter what they do. They can't make me.

When a child shows traits that may be signs of ADHD, we tend to focus almost exclusively on ADHD as the primary explanation for the child's behavioral issues.

We rarely consider the role of anger, and I believe this is a mistake. Anger and resentment are powerful emotions, and I think they definitely contributed to Nicholas' issues. Anyone who has ever experienced anger or resentment knows that these feelings make it harder to focus on your work, exercise self-discipline, think clearly, or remember what's on your to-do list.

When Nicholas came in with his parents, he was encouraged to express what was causing him to feel resentful and angry. Once Nicholas felt he could express his feelings, he seemed to be much more willing to comply with his parents' requests. Effectively, the weight of his anger was lifted.

Callie and Kyle Have PAD ("Pain Avoidance Disorder")

Another feature I've observed in the landscape of modern childhood is something I have come to call *"PAD"* or *"Pain Avoidance Disorder."* A child who is looking to avoid pain or discomfort at all costs will go to enormous lengths to hold on to their pleasure. For these children, a directive to do a basic task or chore is viewed as a huge imposition, and they will go to great lengths to sidestep the perceived discomfort.

Take Callie, a nine-year-old who begged her mother for two years to get a dog. About three months after getting a dog, the novelty wore off. When her parents asked Callie to take the dog out, the request annoyed her, as she was only interested in staying on TikTok or YouTube.

As much as Callie loved her dog, she experienced dog-related chores as painful because they pulled her away from more enjoyable things. So, she did everything she could to avoid basic dog-owner responsibilities.

Children with *PAD* also have interesting notions about school: they seem to think that school should be entirely fun and pleasurable, like the board game Candyland, where each classroom or subject is a different kind of sweet treat. When school is inevitably not fun, boredom kicks in, followed by resistance to and avoidance of school.

To illustrate further, not too long ago fourteen-year-old Kyle offered me a litany of complaints about the horror of school and why he hated it so much. "It's so boring! It's not fun! The teachers are mean and annoying!"

Teasing him in feigned astonishment, I exclaimed, "Wait! Stop. I can't listen anymore. You're delusional. When was school ever fun? Since at least the sixteen-hundreds, school has always been a pain in the rear end." (Although I used the PG-13 term.) "Why should it be any different now?" I asked him.

I asked Kyle to translate to see if he understood what I said.

"School sucks and it's always sucked," Kyle translated.

"Brilliant analysis," I told him with delight.

With a laugh, he went on to tell me why his teachers were a horror, and his classes were terrible. In his telling, his problems were all due to the teachers and the way they ran their classes.

Kyle did not want to face the day-to-day pain of school. Rather than deal with his responsibilities, he preferred blaming his teachers as a way of trying to get out of his schoolwork.

I tried to explain to Kyle that from middle school through high school, students will have about five or six teachers each year. The law of averages tells us that one or two will be quite good, two will be fair, and one will be weak or poor. It's just the way it is.

I try to help kids in Kyle's situation become aware that there's a built-in structure to school, with teachers effectively in charge.

Understanding the law of averages is an important step that helps them get over their school-related hurdles.

Abbey, Age 6, Says "I Have Anger Issues"— Or Perhaps It's Just the Word "No"

One of my favorite kids, Abbey, came in to see me one day.

At the time, Abbey was a recently turned six-year-old starting the first grade in the fall. I had been seeing her since she was three years old and in preschool, and her parents would tell me stories about her daily behavior.

As the mental health professionals like to say, Abbey has issues with "behavioral self-regulation." Abbey's so-called "issues" usually took the form of her not keeping her hands to herself and melting down frequently when things did not go her way.

The day that Abbey came in for an update she chatted about summer camp, which was just starting. She told me that there was a counselor in her bunk specifically assigned to her "because of [her] anger issues."

Abbey's frank statement about her "anger issues" caught me off guard and took me aback a bit. I raised an inquisitive eyebrow and asked her in a somewhat teasing tone, "Oh, yeah? What are your anger issues?"

With a sly smile, Abbey said nothing, but shrugged as if to say, "I don't know. I really don't have any."

My guess is that she really didn't feel like she had any "anger issues." To encourage her further, I asked Abbey to draw pictures of her anger issues. Abbey drew pictures of her friends and the games they played. She loved drawing, but I did not see much content that could indicate any anger.

I complimented her on the drawing, and she smiled widely at me.

While I am not dismissing the idea that young children can have legitimate anger issues, a considerable percentage of children like Abbey may not have "anger issues" even though their behavior and interactions may look like they do.

My interpretation of Abbey's "anger issues" was simple: when she does not get what she wants, Abbey gets angry. In short, Abbey, like the children mentioned previously, has great difficulty with the word "no."

So, as a way of dealing with the dreaded word, "no," Abbey has latched on to the notion that she has "issues." She understands that her behavior is a way to control the key adults in her life.

Jacob, Chloe & Mark Have "F.I.D." ("Frustration Intolerance Disorder")

A variant of the "Pain Avoidance Disorder" mentioned earlier is something I call *"Frustration Intolerance Disorder"* or *FID*.

FID manifests in many ways, and chief among them are meltdowns and spasmodic fits or extreme tantrums when the child encounters even mild frustration. This frustration may stem from sources like homework, but it can also arise from video games, sports, or any other activity that may involve some challenge or difficulty.

Take Jacob, age eight, who thinks of himself as an especially talented athlete. Jacob has been told how talented he is many times, as he's frequently told by his parents that he is nothing short of "amazing." As the firstborn child, his parents have watched his every swing and shot and praised him lavishly for his successes that they dutifully witnessed.

However, as inevitably happens in any sport, there will be missed shots, strikeouts, or other such moments of failure.

Jacob is not equipped to handle these moments. For instance, Jacob and his dad recently went to a pitch and putt golf course. Of course, Jacob's sense of self was such that he thought he would sink virtually every putt that he made.

But after he missed two holes, Jacob had a display of FID, throwing himself on the ground, melting down, crying, and pounding his fists. Trying to console Jacob, his dad did his best to settle him down by telling him he was wonderful and "amazing."

If Jacob and his parents continue doing what they are doing, it will become a cycle—Jacob will continue thinking he should never encounter failure or is somehow too good to fail and that he should never lose a game.

Then, when he inevitably does fail, he will continue seeking reaffirmation of his quasi-superhuman status from his parents, who will continue providing it because they don't want to break the terrible news that he's going to fail sometimes, like everyone else.

Let's also look at Chloe, age six, who overreacts to everything, also showing consistent signs of FID.

For example, if Chloe's father puts her in her car seat and jostles her slightly beyond what she expects, she starts to cry and scream that her dad hurt her on purpose. Profusely apologizing to Chloe, her dad tries to calm her down and help her regain a sense of composure.

Some may say Chloe has "sensory issues" and that's why she reacts like she does. I'm not so sure about that. Chloe rarely shows these behaviors in school or in other interactions outside of the home, suggesting that these are not as beyond her control as the "sensory issues" label would indicate.

FID can also show up in adolescents, not just young kids.

For instance, Mark, aged fifteen, is tied to his game system about four or five hours a day. Completing schoolwork is almost never on his mind. Frequently, Mark has meltdowns in his basement while he plays. These meltdowns can get violent and out of control with extreme fits of rage.

The other night, while his parents were upstairs, Mark had a meltdown. Cursing, throwing his game controller against the wall, and nearly putting his fist through the drywall, Mark repeatedly screamed, "I fucking suck! I fucking suck!"

When his parents tried to calm him down, they found Mark inconsolable.

These FID kids are not easy, and in many ways, their struggles are heightened by our current child-rearing philosophy of not allowing kids to face frustration, as well as an over-preoccupation for their self-esteem.

This concern about self-esteem can lead to an emphasis on making sure the child feels totally positive in every possible situation—including situations when it's natural or even healthy for them to feel somewhat negative.

There is no quick fix or solution for FID, but later on, we'll talk about how adopting a matter-of-fact parenting style and attitude can help your child become more capable of dealing with frustration.

"But I've Got FOMO"

Emerson, a sixteen-year-old boy I work with, used his parents' credit card inappropriately. Specifically, he took the card without permission and bought a video game to play with his friends. Emerson's parents were rightfully upset about this.

When I asked Emerson how his thought process ran as he was making these decisions, he said sheepishly, "I don't know. I think I'm impulsive and have FOMO. Do you know what that is? I think I was afraid of missing out on having fun with my friends."

(In case you don't know, "FOMO" is a slang term for "Fear of Missing Out.")

I stared back at him in bewilderment, and I let some seconds go by.

Then, in a teasing style, without skipping a beat, I nearly shouted, "FOMO! Impulsive! Don't hand me that utter horse shit! Please stop blowing smoke up my ass!" (Yes, that's what I said.) "And where did you get that word, 'impulsive'? Where'd you come up with that? Do you know what impulsive means?"

Laughing, but somewhat stunned, Emerson muttered, "What do you mean I don't have FOMO?"

"You don't have FOMO," I said. "You have a very different disorder."

Now I'd piqued Emerson's attention. "Really?" he said curiously. "What disorder do I have?"

"You have a bad case of '*IWWIWD*,'" I said.

"I never heard of that disorder. What is that? Is it related to ADD?" asked Emerson.

"No. It has nothing to do with ADD," I told him. "IWWIWD is a disorder that plagues many American kids. This disorder leads them to do stupid things like take their parents' credit cards. IWWIWD is 'I Want What I Want Disorder.'"

I continued, "To be more accurate, it's 'I Want What I Want When I Want It Disorder,' but it's shortened a bit to IWWIWD. You can look it up in the psychology books," I said jokingly.

At that point Emerson fell out of his chair laughing. As his reaction told me, I had hit him squarely between the eyes, and he knew it. Emerson was already well aware that he had a bad case of IWWIWD.

If you're the parent of a child who has IWWIWD, try and stay away from the more clinical explanations for your child's behavior ("The poor baby is so impulsive because of his ADD"). Instead, as you start to shift your parenting attitude, you will see this "disorder" for what it is, and you'll have quite a different reaction to the behavior.

Turning Down the PNQ
(Parent Nag Quotient)

Whether you're a parent with kids still under your roof or your children are grown, here's a question for you. When you make comments or ask questions like the following, what kind of responses do you get?

"Why haven't you started your homework?"

"How come you never pay attention?"

"All you do is whine and complain! Just get started!"

"Your room's a mess. I'm sick of picking up after you."

"You and your sister are fighting again! Why can't we ever have a peaceful dinner?"

"I told you before we got to the store to not run ahead, and you completely ignored me! Why don't you listen?"

"All you do is play Fortnite. I'm sick of you playing video games."

"Why are you ignoring me all the time?"

Once your child is about ten, they've probably heard thousands of similar comments, questions, or complaints from you. But has your child ever said any of the following?

"Gee, Mom, you're right. I should start my homework. Thanks for reminding me."

"Yes, my room is a chaotic mess, and it will be good for me to put my things away."

"I love my sister, and I know that we are disrupting dinner, so we will be more supportive of each other from now on."

"You know, Dad, I have been overly addicted to playing Fortnite, and I will start reducing my video game playing time so I can focus better on my schoolwork."

"You're right, Mom. I disregarded you when we went to the store last time, and I will walk by your side today."

Even though nagging and pecking never produce the desired result, it is the number one go-to strategy used by parents everywhere. (It's followed closely by yelling.) This nagging goes on and on with no positive result. There must be more effective alternatives—we've seen some of them in this book. So why do we do it?

Maybe you've spent a lot of time, breath, and energy nagging your kids over the years, and it's tough to think of all those wasted resources.

But now is the time to admit that nagging has no impact. And now is the time to turn down the Parent Nag Quotient, or PNQ. You'll be glad you did. Later on, we'll review a parenting strategy that gives you a much more effective alternative to nagging.

"Hey, Bud. How About We Get Ready for Bed?"

On a recent HBO special, the comedian Bill Maher spent part of his comic observations focusing on modern children and their parents.

Maher said something like, "First of all, where did parents get the idea that they have to negotiate with their kids? I see this in the way they speak to their kids: 'Hey, Buddy. Are you ready to go?'" Maher said this mockingly, then continued. "When we were kids, it wasn't like that. It was, 'Get in the (expletive) car.'"

I knew immediately what Maher meant.

As I mentioned earlier, psychology began to overemphasize children's self-esteem many years ago, so kids are frequently coddled by their parents to the point where we are worried that if we put undue stress or demands on them, they will break like fragile teacups.

In some ways, kids are not that complicated. While they certainly seek love and approval, what do you think is the number one underlying driver for most kids?

What do they seek virtually all the time? Self-esteem? Sounds nice, but no.

So, what do kids want? An expression from my Granny's day can answer this question. "They just want to have their bread buttered on both sides," Granny would say.

In other words, they want to have it their way, with no frustration: pleasure around the clock. And when kids seek pleasure all the time and do end up having their bread buttered on both sides, they often become hedonistic pirates!

Here is one recent example of a very young hedonist who is parented in the "Hey, Bud" style.

I was in a pediatrician's office, waiting for a patient of mine to arrive. Seated nearby was a dad with his child, who looked about five. The child crashed around the waiting room recklessly, and his dad ignored him. Then the child started to walk, or stomp, on the waiting room chairs.

I admit I was appalled.

The dad did not seem to care much, but at some point, in a very friendly tone, he said, "Hey, Bud, why don't you come over here?"

But the child ignored his father and continued to stomp on the chairs.

Inherent in the "Hey, Bud" style of communication is the philosophy that drives the manner and way you speak to the child. This philosophy is based on the belief that being the child's friend and interacting with them on that level will benefit the child and improve their self-esteem.

Enhancing self-esteem or self-concept has been a central preoccupation of modern parents, who believe that a child with adequate or high self-esteem will be able to tackle most challenges, both academic and social.

Over the last twenty-five years, schools have also embraced this philosophy regarding teacher-child interaction. This shift is also grounded in the notion that if children feel good about themselves, all will be well.

My guess is that the dad described above probably believed that his child was expressing his personal creativity as he ran on the waiting room chairs. This dad may have thought that if he limited his son and set clear boundaries, he would stifle him.

There is a difference, though, between having fun, engaging in all kinds of play, and being the child's friend with no limits. Friendships should be equal: no one in the relationship should have legitimate authority over the other.

But since you are your child's parent, there will always be a power imbalance between the two of you. What's more, your authority is legitimate and inherent. This means that a parent-child relationship will always be different from friendship.

It is my sense that parents have become increasingly uncomfortable with the inherent power imbalance in a parent-child relationship. By believing that being their child's friend will cultivate their child's self-esteem, they diminish their own authority in a futile attempt to create an equal relationship.

Marianne: "Not Doing What My Parents Did to Me"

Frequently our parenting style is driven by a promise to ourselves that we will not do to our children what our parents did to us. We may not want to repeat parenting strategies used by the previous generation that we consider inappropriate or harmful.

To illustrate this, let's look at Marianne, whose daughter, Vivian, is a difficult five-year-old.

Marianne once explained her own upbringing this way, "My parents were very old school in a 1950s kind of way. My dad was very stern and strict, rarely soft and warm, while my mom was always nice, in an overly cheerful way. They yelled a lot at my sister and me."

"We were always being punished and told what to do," Marianne continued. "We were never encouraged to be independent or to think on our own. I think I always struggled with my own self-concept, as they were extremely critical. I still struggle with self-doubt and easily get down on myself, especially in relation to my own kids and my style of parenting."

"I think their parenting had a big impact on my thinking and my philosophy of parenting. From the beginning, I told myself that I would parent differently. I would not raise them sternly or harshly.

"Unfortunately, I think the pendulum has swung too far in the other direction. My five-year-old has significant and frequent meltdowns. She can be quite demanding, always wanting things to go the way she wants.

"Others see her as very inflexible and oppositional. I find her to be a constant challenge. My own parents are extremely critical of how I raise my kids. I honestly don't know what the right thing is to do."

Underneath Marianne's words is a considerable discomfort with being authoritative or in charge. To many parents like Marianne, *authoritative* parenting reminds them of the *authoritarian* style that was so pervasive in earlier generations. Such a style counters their core belief, from a psychological standpoint, about what children need.

The clues to this discomfort with being authoritative are usually evident in parents' words and body language. Their language is laced with hesitancy yet conveys a desire to over-explain things. For instance, Vivian screams at Marianne when it is bedtime. She says, "I'm not tired! I don't want to go to bed."

As the screaming ensues, Marianne speaks in quiet tones to explain the rationale for sleep. "Honey," she starts, "You know you need your rest. So does mommy. We all need our sleep. You know how hard it is to function in school when you don't get your sleep. Sleep is important for all our health."

Vivian buys none of what her mom says, and she continues to scream and make demands. Her mother's explanations have no impact on Vivian whatsoever. Yet whenever she can, Marianne tries this strategy to counter virtually all of Vivian's challenging behaviors.

Similar interactions take place in Vivian's preschool. It's common for Vivian to get into arguments with her classmates when she does not get what she wants.

Vivian's nice teacher frequently confers with Marianne, and they develop different strategies to help Vivian get along better with her classmates. Mostly, these strategies involve putting smiley faces or stickers on a behavior chart whenever she does something appropriate.

Vivian doesn't seem to care very much about the stickers or the smiley faces.

While the school's staff do not state it directly and even though they often remind Marianne that "We're not doctors," they convey the message that Vivian should be evaluated for ADHD.

Vivian's pediatrician vehemently disagrees with this thought process, and she considers Vivian's issues to be "all behavioral and not medical."

Now that I've observed Vivian, I have to agree.

Walking in the Mud

Let's say you are walking with your six-year-old and four-year-old around a soccer field that is muddy on the perimeter from a recent heavy rainfall. You ask your children not to walk in the mud. The four-year-old blatantly defies you and walks straight into the mud, with all the expected results.

What do you do? How do you handle it? A common reaction would be to simply yell at the child to jolt him out of it and to express your displeasure. In this situation, it would probably not be the worst thing to do.

But here's a more proactive approach.

Get on eye level with your child and speak in clear, objective tones, saying something like this: "I asked you not to walk in the mud. I am giving you one more warning. This was supposed to be fun. You do it one more time, and we go straight home. No TV, iPad—nothing. It will be quiet time."

In this second approach, you do not express anger. You take charge, and the consequence is a natural one that is built into the situation. Then the next time you are planning a trip to this same field, a straightforward conversation like the following would help to put the odds in your favor.

"Remember the last time we went to the muddy field? Well, we're going again today, and there may be muddy spots. You know I do not want you running through the mud. What will happen if you do it again?

"We go right home."

"Correct. It's your call how you want it to go, but remember, no screen time if we turn around."

I predict there will be no mud walking.

This is a proactive and direct approach that will be expanded upon further.

"A Big Bowl of..."

A frustrated mom named Jan reduced her son's challenges to the most basic terms. As she spoke to me about her twelve-year-old sixth grader, Jackson, she went through a list of his issues:

+ Resistant to homework
+ Hates reading
+ Frequent meltdowns
+ Constant YouTubing
+ Disrespectful to his parents
+ Sees school as pointless
+ Seemingly no motivation
+ No sustained effort
+ Low tolerance for any difficulty or frustration

Two different physicians had diagnosed Jackson with ADHD and taking a common approach, they signed off on a prescription and told Jan to start Jackson on the medication and check back with them in four months.

As Jan reported, the medication seemed to help some for maybe two or three weeks, when Jackson appeared mildly more focused and compliant. However, Jan now offered a more accurate and simple description. As she noted, "It's just a big bowl of shit!"

That's about the size of it. We seem to want to ascribe specific categories or labels to this big bowl, but this is challenging: there is no x-ray or hard scientific measurement to indicate that a child has this one condition or the other. Yet I hear these labels all the time from parents:

"She has a sensory disorder."

"My child has ADHD."

"Yes, it's dyslexia."

On and on it goes with the listing of disorders and attempts to utilize single, neurobiological explanations for a child's complex, yet ordinary struggles.

Today, for instance, I spoke with a cute and endearing eight-year-old girl, Maria, who has had difficulty being accepted by her peer group in school. Instead of discussing ADHD or Maria's "possible sensory issues" with the mom and the girl, I tried to help Maria understand the skill of getting along with others.

We spoke about how she can "go over the top" and not read the signals.

When I asked her to play back what I said to her, to discern whether she heard me, she said, "I try too hard to be cool, and it can get annoying and get on people's nerves."

"Bingo!"

In Maria's case, focusing on the skill of thinking through social encounters will probably be much more productive than overemphasizing a theoretical neurobiological disorder.

So, back to Jan and the "big bowl of shit:" experiences like hers, Jackson's, and Maria's have shown me something valuable that I like to share with parents.

I've seen that breaking a child's issues down in terms of the skills they have and the skills they need to develop is probably a lot more effective than "disorder thinking."

Gum and Candy at 7:30 a.m.

It's early in the morning. Breakfast hasn't yet been served. You have made it clear that gum and candy are not to be had in the morning. You inadvertently left some candy and gum in a bowl on the table.

Out of the corner of your eye, you see your six-year-old unravel a pack of candy. You know his nature. If you stop him or take the gum away, he will have a meltdown. You need to get your kids ready for school and do not want to deal with any of it. What are your choices? What do you do?

First off, you need to recognize that you'll meet some level of defiance. A point needs to be made. Letting the child have the candy gives the wrong message. Your best option is to take the candy away and speak in clear, direct terms. If a meltdown occurs, so be it. An additional statement that "all candy is put away until you learn to follow the rules" would not hurt.

Now when it comes to preventing future recurrences, I tell parents that "tuck-in time" is a good time to review some of the events from the day. In this situation, you can have a rules-clarification discussion regarding the morning routine.

"Now what's the rule about candy in the morning?" you might ask.

"We're not allowed to have any."

"Correct. And what will happen if you do?"

"Mommy will get very upset, and I will lose some privileges."

"Correct again. Brilliant!"

Again, what do you predict will happen?

Fourth of July Controversy

Your family settles in at a local park to watch the Fourth of July fireworks in a school field. As the five-year-old notices a relatively small branch that hangs overhead, she becomes insistent that the branch will block her view of the fireworks. You and your wife have explained to her that the fireworks will fill up the big sky, and the branch will not block her view.

Remaining insistent, she becomes increasingly upset, convinced that "it's all terrible" and she won't be able to see anything.

She works herself up into a crying jag. You look around and think maybe you could oblige her, but there really is no choice, as families have settled in on blankets all around yours.

What are your options?

Some people might try to placate the child and continue with rational explanations, or they might try to move to another area, even though finding a different spot is a long shot at this point. In this case, completely ignoring the child ("active ignoring") might be the choice that best reflects a proactive parenting attitude.

The only caveat to this approach is that the child's crying and potential meltdown may be a disturbance to others. If this becomes the case, then either you or your wife must sacrifice the view of the fireworks and take her away from the situation. It would be fundamentally unfair to your other child if the whole family were to pack up and go because the five-year-old held you hostage.

Lighting Matches in the Basement

I once met an eight-year-old, Ethan, who started lighting matches in the basement because he thought that it looked "pretty cool." His dad, a cerebral type, scratched his head while his son told the story, then stated, "Well, I guess it's an expression of how Ethan feels. I guess he's angry about something."

What do you think?

Much like Ethan's father, some parents can be overly intellectual in their analysis of child behavior. If Ethan's dad had followed his well-intentioned but over-intellectual theory, Ethan would be looking at a serious psychiatric evaluation, which is not a pleasant experience, plus a possible misdiagnosis with a very severe condition.

The reality was, however, that as you talked to Ethan and his dad, the dad realized that he had been overly hasty in jumping to theoretical conclusions. Ethan really did just think the matches looked cool.

All Ethan actually required was a firm talking-to about how he was never to light matches without supervision until he was much older, plus a time-out and loss of privileges that was a reasonable consequence for his behavior. This outcome was much more appropriate than being treated as a budding pyromaniac or arsonist.

Won't Get Out of the Car

Ryan and his sister are being taken to visit their grandmother, who has recently been released from the hospital after minor surgery. As they leave, Ryan expresses excitement and enthusiasm about the visit.

However, when they pull into his grandmother's driveway, something clearly shifts. Curled into a ball, Ryan refuses to get out of the car, as he won't have access to his iPad once he gets inside.

Because he is normally a challenging child, Ryan's mom knows the basic signs, and she knows that if she pushes him, a full-blown meltdown will ensue. Caught between a rock and a hard place, she is unsure what to do. She had hoped that seeing the grandkids would help lift her mother's spirits, but with Ryan's mood and negative grunting in the backseat, she is not so sure. Now, for whatever reason that Ryan cannot express, he cannot go along with the program.

So how does this end?

Ryan's mom wants to try to coax or "reward" him for getting out of the car. But Grandma has the better idea: she sits on the front porch in full view of the car, completely ignoring Ryan. She knows that any other approach would fuel the fire.

A Case of the "Didjas"

Modern parenting is plagued by a bad case of the "Didjas." (i.e., "Did you do such-and-such a thing?")

While the content may vary somewhat, here are some common Didjas:

- "Didja start your homework?"
- "Didja finish your homework?"
- "Didja put your stuff away?"
- "Didja brush your teeth?"
- "Didja take out the trash?"
- "Didja get out of bed?"
- "Didja put your lunch in your bookbag?"
- "Didja remember your equipment for practice today?"

On and on it goes.

Guess what's happening inside the typical kid's head while he's being didja'd to death? That's right, his eyeballs roll back into his skull while he mutters a range of unpleasant statements, laced with occasional barely audible and well-aimed curses.

Morning Rituals

In the Sterling household, their two teenage boys, age sixteen and fourteen, along with their twelve-year-old girl, have taken over the household in the mornings, to the point where the parents only long to escape and go somewhere else.

Every night, the parents tell me, the kids stay up too late to play on the Xbox and then need to be dragged out of bed. When the mom tries to make breakfast for them, they scream in protest while they text their friends and check YouTube, tuning their parents out. They ignore their parents' questions about school. But their yelling at, arguing with, and provoking each other is by far the worst part of the whole morning experience. Overall, the tensions run deep.

The problem here is that it is largely forgotten or not understood that screen time (i.e., phones, iPads, TV, gaming systems) is a privilege, not a necessity. Most kids are incredibly connected or even addicted to these devices.

The one silver lining, though, is that these devices offer parents considerable leverage.

Before the Sterling parents spoke to me, they had harangued and yelled at their kids with no impact. But I suggested they try a matter-of-fact conversation like the following—I think it's a pretty sure bet to resolve the issue with minimal effort.

As you sit your kids down for a family meeting, you state in calm and clear tones: "Listen, your father and I need to talk to you about something. We are very distressed in the morning. The yelling, arguing, and negativity have gotten out of hand. On a scale of one to ten, with ten being the worst, it's a nine or ten every morning.

"Here's the deal. Unless there is going to be more cooperation and basic manners in the morning, everything will be shut off for the remainder of the day. No iPads and no game system, and the phones are put away for the evening. The next day, we will try again. It doesn't matter who started it or who you think is most to blame. Everyone is in it. It's your choice how you want it to go."

That's it.

Trying to get to the root of inter-sibling conflict and determine and appropriately punish the biggest culprit is futile. Make your point and use the kids' devices—or some other much-valued luxury—as leverage. If this results in one more morning of nine- or ten-level negativity, so be it. It will change very soon. I guarantee it.

Held Hostage by an Insomniac

A family recently told me that they had great difficulty with their ten-year-old, Derek, who they said was an "insomniac." He never went to bed without major battles. Getting him off his gaming system was a nightly struggle that always ended with various members of the family screaming at each other.

When I asked how the parents handled it, the mom noted that she had smaller children that she put to bed while Derek played. I asked what the dad did while this happened. "I don't know," she said. "He's in the basement on the internet or on his iPad. I have no idea. I just know he offers no support, and I am exhausted."

Basically, I thought, the dad needs to wake up and understand the impact of his own screen indulgence. I didn't see the child's behavior as the product of insomnia, but of the simple fact that Derek wanted what he wanted: pleasure. It was the same with the dad.

Much like the Sterling kids, Derek needs to know what rules he must follow in exchange for the privilege of using the gaming system. Most parents give access to gaming systems unconditionally, with no rules established. But this is like handing car keys over to a sixteen-year-old and saying, "Here you go." A clear, rules-based conversation with Derek will go a long way to clear up his "insomnia."

2,555 Hours Logged In

Let's say you're north of age 50 or 55. Unless there is an eight-year-old boy in your world, the word Fortnite likely means little to you. But I hear it all the time.

I try to understand the personal landscape of each kid I work with, so I ask what they do with their free time. Boys tell me repeatedly about Fortnite, a video game many say they are *obsessed* with.

Let's take Avery, age eleven, who is an unmotivated fifth grader. I ask him about his day and what he does when he is not in school or in online school.

This is during the COVID-19 pandemic, so he mumbles indistinctly through his mask as he says, "Play Fortnite."

In a slightly teasing tone, I say, "Really? I'm shocked. How many hours do you think you play a day?"

Avery shrugs and mumbles, "Don't know."

I don't let up. "Come on. Let's take a guess. It doesn't have to be exact. On average, how much do you play every day? One? Two? Three hours? Four? More?"

"Maybe about seven," Avery says. Keep in mind that his mom sits by us and does not disagree.

"Seven hours!" I shout for effect. "Do you know how many days are in a year?"

"No," Avery says.

"Well, there are 365 days in a year," I tell him. "So, let's figure out how many hours of Fortnite you play in a year."

I ask Avery to use his phone (yes, an eleven-year-old has a phone) to multiply 365 by 7.

Avery tells me, "2,555 hours."

I continue with my melodramatic shock, although I am not actually that shocked.

I turn to his mom. "Mom, what do you think? About how many hours does he do anything that would represent something like academic work?"

Avery's mom notes that they fight all the time about schoolwork, but it goes nowhere. She says, "At best, he maybe puts in about a half-hour, three or four days a week, but nothing on Friday, Saturday, or Sunday. He never reads."

Turning back to Avery, I say, "OK, so your mom says you put in maybe two hours a week on average with school stuff. There are fifty-two weeks in a year. So, let's multiply fifty-two weeks by two hours on your phone. What's your answer?"

"A hundred and four."

Over 2,000 hours vs. 104, and his parents want to understand why things are going poorly.

Parents, get out your calculators. Set your boundaries. Set the limits.

Sobbing in the Waiting Room

Accompanied by his father Julian, six-year-old Lawrence was sobbing in my waiting room. Clearly, Lawrence was unhappy about being brought in to see me. After he settled into my office—still on the floor though—Lawrence continued to sob and whimper. I basically ignored Lawrence while I spoke with his father.

At some point, Julian stopped the conversation and tried to comfort Lawrence, rubbing his back and asking him what was wrong. He attempted to use some type of reward, such as "We can go to McDonald's after Dr. Rich's," but that was ignored.

Lawrence was having none of it. In fact, the more his dad tried to comfort him, the louder Lawrence wailed. In the middle of trying to comfort Lawrence, I stopped Julian and asked, "What are you doing?"

Bewildered by my question, he responded, "Well, Lawrence is obviously upset. Maybe he's scared."

So, with Lawrence in earshot, I told Julian, "Listen, Lawrence has a choice. He can continue to be unhappy on the floor and cry and whimper, or he can choose to have fun and play with some of the toys while we talk. It's up to him. He'll decide."

Two minutes after that statement, Lawrence happily played on his own, and he did not show anxiety or discomfort. If someone entered the room at this point, they would have had no clue how distraught Lawrence was two minutes before. Lawrence was not scared. He knew me well. He simply wanted to go home so he could get back to what he wanted to do.

So rather than chasing psychological theories and following trails that lead nowhere, it's often better to give the child a choice and leave it up to them.

It's Called "Homework," Not "Homefun"

Lately, I've had a run of "meltdowny" kids. These are the ones who, without much provocation, have a wild storm of a fit. Often, it's tied to something like homework or school-related demands. I'm not sure why, but there seem to be a lot more of them these days.

I recently asked a child about his reaction to homework, and he told me plaintively, "It's just not fun. It's so boring."

I joked with him (sort of), "Hey, it was never fun. It's school!" I'm not sure he was buying it.

"Homework is boring..." he repeated.

Somewhere along the line, kids seem to have gotten the idea that school and homework are supposed to be fun, enjoyable activities that will ignite motivation for learning. Most of the homework that I've seen consists of packets of worksheet after worksheet. The worksheets never look like much fun to me. But then again, they never were.

Perhaps it was the boomer generation, in their post-hippie child-raising period, who invented the notion that homework should be more of an "experience" for children. The current generation of parents has just further embraced the idea that homework should be something that feels positive, so they have very high hopes for how their child's homework will go each night.

It seems that there is some value to homework; it teaches kids to manage their stuff, organize themselves, meet deadlines, and, oh yeah, it reinforces a few academic skills along the way.

Yet probably since Colonial times, kids have detested homework. Think about it: in the history of American education, has there ever been a child who raised their hand at the end of the day and asked, "Please, could we have an extra hour or two of homework tonight, or more on the weekend?"

And why have Saturdays always been beloved by kids? Easy. No one bugs them to get stuff done. No homework.

So, the next time your child has a meltdown about homework that's "no fun and so boring," shrug your shoulders, stay calm, and have a ready response, such as, "That's right, honey, it's called 'homework.' They don't call it 'homefun.'"

If your child persists and raises their meltdown to another level of intensity, go about your business. You know, take out the trash, do the dishes. Do anything to disengage, and the storm will pass.

After the meltdown is over and the child resets themselves, approach them again. Skip the usual reactive parental add-ons like nagging, yelling, or punishment. Instead, simply say, "Are you ready to start now?"

A meltdown is like a storm, and like a storm, it passes.

Summary

One of the biggest differences between children and adults (at least in theory), is that adults are able to put aside their immediate desire for pleasure to do tasks, chores or to meet responsibilities. While these may not be fun, adults know that pleasure and fun are not always immediately accessible.

Many children are also able to do this. They face responsibility and put aside their immediate desire for pleasure or fun. Homework is fully representative of this, as homework almost never would be thought of as fun. However, flexible children tend to roll up their sleeves and get down to business. This flexible style shows up in many other places, such as getting ready for bed and putting clothes away.

Group B children seek pleasure at all costs, wanting to hold on to pleasure and not face reality that is impinging upon them. Like slot machine players who pull the lever repeatedly in the hope of getting a positive response, the meltdowns and demands try and get a hit, such as staying up later and not getting off the iPad. If there are ten meltdowns that yield one hit, then that is a sort of a victory, like when playing slot machines.

The children of concern have great difficulty coping and are frequently viewed through the lens of disorders and a lack of emotional self-regulation. Difficulty coping and regulating their emotions are among the hallmark indicators of these types of children.

THE LANDSCAPE OF PARENTING

In this section we set our sights on the landscape of parenting. The way you view parenting will shape your attitudes and decisions, and these will ultimately make a great deal of difference with your child.

And from the outset, I want to make it clear that no part of this discussion is meant to place blame on or criticize any parent. Parenting is always challenging. Parenting challenging children is even more so.

When it comes to managing difficult children, there is no one formula or answer. Everyone's situation differs and individual circumstances must be considered.

Some parents, for example, are single moms with little support. Others may be in a contentious marriage or in a situation that is adversarial and finger-pointing when it comes to raising the children. Some may have several children living in a relatively small physical space.

Each family's circumstances shape the individual's needs, the family's priorities, and parenting decisions. The factors that may be contributing to a child's behavior are literally endless, each one requiring an understanding of the circumstances when considering what to do.

As I mentioned in the last section while recounting Jennifer's story, it is my impression that moms, much more so than dads, often end up criticizing and blaming themselves when things do not go well with their child. To the moms reading this, I encourage you, to the extent you can, to try and turn down the self-critical voice.

A Pie Chart of Variables

Here's a perspective that I find helpful in navigating the challenging landscape of parenting.

Whenever I talk to parents, I find myself reminding them that there is typically a pie chart of variables contributing to the child's current behaviors and situation.

As we discussed in the previous section, temperament is a big piece of the pie. Along with temperament, family dynamics, parenting styles, and the child's neuro-developmental situation all impact their behavior. Also in the pie chart is your child's social-emotional growth, the influence of peers and other adults, and the ideas they encounter through school and the media. Keeping the pie chart in mind helps give parents perspective, and it typically takes the edge off any excessive self-criticism.

Remembering the pie chart can also help parents who may be wondering, "Is it this or that?" (As in, does their child have ADHD or something else.) As I like to tell them, it's "this *and* that."

Often, it's "this and that and that…"

Taking Inventory

With that said, a good first step is for you to take inventory of your parenting style or characteristic attitude in terms of how you typically address challenging behaviors.

While taking stock of yourself as a parent, here are some questions to consider that will help you to know where you stand:

- Am I too soft?
- Too tough?
- Am I indulgent?
- Do I yell too much?
- Do I tend to be impatient?
- Am I over-worrying?
- Do I hover too much?
- Am I afraid to be a person of authority?
- Am I embracing currently popular parenting philosophies that contribute to my child's problems?
- How involved are my extended family members and what are their roles? Are any of them too involved and overly opinionated?

The potential questions are endless, but these are some of the major ones. Use them to help get you started but try to come up with more questions on your own.

So, let's survey the landscape and look at some common parenting styles.

Parenting Styles

So how might you describe your primary parenting style?

There are a variety of common styles. And as in the case of Group A and Group B children, there is no one test or absolute marker that can place you in one category or another—but you will probably be able to recognize yourself in at least one of the descriptions below. Most parents have one style or a combination of two, with one predominating.

Before going any further, though, it is important to clarify what I mean by the word "style" in this context. As I view it, parenting style is a combination of the parent's characteristic way of talking to a child, the typical tone they use, and their body language. These factors largely characterize the way a parent interacts.

In other words, one's primary style conveys one's particular attitude of parenting.

Our parenting styles are largely something we have observed and learned from our own parents, or they may be linked to our particular personality types.

While I do not think that a parent can change their style completely, I strongly believe that a modification in style can make considerable positive differences in the child's behavior.

So, in no particular order, here are the common styles.

Pushover Parents

A prevalent style of modern parenting is what I call Pushover Parenting. Pushover Parents continually make compromises in the attempt to keep the peace and encourage greater reasonableness on the part of the child.

While compromise can certainly be a great thing to teach children, with this style of parenting, children learn early on that they can get what they want if they become more demanding and insistent.

One of the telling characteristics of pushover parents is that they negotiate to a fault with their child to get them to cooperate. For example, they might regularly say things like, "OK, you can play another half-hour of video games if you promise to get ready for bed after."

Pushover Parents also convey a great deal of doubt and insecurity in their tone and way of speaking. This insecurity is often what leads the child to start taking advantage of the parent at an early age.

Parents may adopt this parenting style with good intentions: they were often raised by stricter, more demanding parents who they considered overly harsh. In effect, Pushover Parents decide early on that they are not going to treat their children the same way their parents treated them. While this may be a worthwhile goal, they end up going too far in the other direction.

"Hey, Bud" Parents

A slight variation on the Pushover Parent is the "Hey, Bud" Parent. By describing their child as their "buddy," this parent strives to be the child's friend above all, so they downplay the more authoritative aspects of parenting.

Underlying this style is the belief that being a friend to the child helps them feel good about themselves, and the child will then behave appropriately. These parents sincerely believe that this approach serves their child's best interests and supports their psychological well-being.

This parenting belief has a clear origin.

A long time ago, in a galaxy far away, parents of a very different generation frequently used the phrase, "Because I said so" when their child questioned why they needed to do something they did not want to do.

There was no negotiation or explanation. It was simply, "Because I said so."

This phrase became unpopular with parents of the subsequent generation, who found it harsh, dismissive, psychologically inappropriate, and likely to shut down parent-child communication.

This "dated" way of talking to children was then largely replaced by a communication style that put parents and children on more equal footing—hence the negotiations used by Pushover Parents and hence "Hey, Bud."

As in the case of Pushover Parents, "Hey, Bud" parents can be identified by the way they speak to their children.

Let's say it's about 7:00 p.m. and a challenging eight-year-old has been playing about four hours of video games and hasn't started any homework. The child's father might say in a tentative voice, "Hey, Bud, how about we start to do our homework?" Do you predict that talking this way will convince the challenging child to stop playing video games and start homework?

That's not a bet I would take.

This phrase conveys little in the way of authority—it's a weak, questioning manner of speaking. Like we saw in the case of Amelia and Andrea, children can become contemptuous of adults who use this communication style. And just like with Pushover Parenting, some children readily learn to double down on their demands.

In addition, the phrase "our homework" is problematic. Remember that it's never "*our* homework." It's your *child's* homework. In fact, in the real-life scenario I described, the eight-year-old went right on playing his video games while completely ignoring his father.

After another twenty minutes or so of video games, he completed his homework halfheartedly in a very disconnected way, then went right back to the gaming console. The father was frustrated but did not convey this to the child.

The "Hey, Bud" approach does not usually result in much compliance.

Psychological Theories Parents

Even though I'm a psychologist, many psychological explanations that parents offer to explain their child's behavior don't sit well with me.

Often these parents may have consulted medical or other psychological practitioners, or they may have done a lot of reading about the issues. It's not that the information itself is necessarily unsound.

The problem arises when parents become reliant on single-factor explanations, as in "the diagnosis." The focus on "the diagnosis" (whether it's ADHD or another condition) leads parents into single factor thinking.

In other words, they view the diagnosis or the label as the sole reason or explanation for the child's behavior, when in fact there are many other interacting variables that go beyond the child's psychological or neurological condition.

Here are some other examples of psychological theories that parents frequently use as single explanations for their child's behavior:

- As the child has a full-blown defiant meltdown, the parent interprets the behavior as being due to "sensory needs" without considering alternatives.
- While the child grabs other children's toys, the parent says, "He has trouble with self-regulation."
- A four-year-old refuses to lie down during class nap time, and the parent explains, "Her anxiety takes over and she can't settle in during nap time." (Here, I sometimes ask, "Her anxiety makes her ignore you?")
- "Well, she can't do her homework for more than five minutes because of her ADD." (There is nothing that says children with ADD literally cannot do homework.)
- "He's a little on the spectrum side, and no one likes him," a parent says to explain the child's lack of friends. (Just

because a child is having negative social interactions does not mean they must be autistic.)

Again, many children have legitimate psychological or neurological issues that should not be ignored. But the tricky thing about a diagnosis is that once the child receives some type of label, that label can become the narrative that underlies the child's behavior.

There's also a concern unique to ADHD/ADD: these diagnoses are frequently offered for a range of behaviors including homework refusal, disregarding rules, throwing tantrums, and a whole host of others. And as we've seen, for many children these behaviors are not related to ADHD/ADD at all.

As noted in a *Psychology Today* article on ADHD. By Keith Conners, the so-called "Father of ADHD:"

The history of psychiatry has always been a history of fads... What is new now is the massive commercialization of psychiatric disorders in the service of pharmaceutical profit-selling the ill through non-stop disease mongering in order to peddle the pill. Harried doctors and worried patients have bought into the medicalization of everyday life, turning distress and difference into mental disorder.

The diagnosis of ADHD should be a last resort, not an automatic reflex or attempt at a quick fix. Information should come from careful direct observation and from a wide array of well-informed informants. Evaluations should stretch over weeks or months because kids can change so much from visit to visit.

Democratic Parents

According to multiple theories of family therapy, the family has a natural, built-in hierarchy. But as in the case of Pushover Parents, some younger parents do not share this understanding of family dynamics—they're uncomfortable with the notion of a parent at the top of a hierarchy.

These parents may adopt the Democratic Style of parenting, in which everyone in the family—regardless of age and level of maturity—has an equal say in what takes place each day.

A family in which the children are running the show creates many issues. Effectively, the tail is wagging the dog. These families have little to no apparent hierarchy.

A classic example is bedtime. While there will always be a little wiggle-room in terms of negotiating bedtime, Democratic Style seeks input from the children as to want time they want to go to bed or feel like getting off their iPads. This is a recipe for disaster.

Over-Involved, Hovering Parents

Parents are vulnerable to anxiety, and this can cause them to develop an over-involved parenting style. These parents are sometimes referred to as "lawnmower parents" because their intent is to make things smoother and easier for their child. Others have referred to them as "helicopter parents" for their continual hovering.

Regardless of whether they are mowing or hovering, these over-involved parents want to ensure that their child feels little frustration, so they do everything in their power to make things nice and easy.

For instance, they are always logging on to view their child's school assignments, reminding the child of the work they have not done. This prevents their child from experiencing negative consequences at school.

However, their attempts to protect their child from frustration often backfire when their child becomes frustrated *with them.*

For example, Zachary, age fourteen, tells me he is angry and resentful of his parents because they interfere with him too often. I ask him to elaborate.

"They never let up," Zachary tells me. "It's constant. If I miss one assignment, I hear about it immediately, and then they threaten to take away my phone and to shut down my game system. We fight all the time. They are always in my face."

As I think about this parenting style, I remember when my son was about thirteen and I started to ask him a lot of questions about what he did or did not do in school. I became annoyed at him for not being more forthcoming and straightforward, and my irritation was obvious.

Becoming frustrated as well, he said, "Let me ask you this, Dad. Did you tell *your* parents everything about school and your assignments? On a day-to-day basis, did they really know what you were doing?"

That stopped me in my tracks. I had to be honest. My answer was definite: "No. They had no idea." And my dad was a school principal!

We cannot return to a time before we could use cell phones, the internet, and GPS tracking to constantly monitor what our kids are doing. But technology isn't the problem—the gadgets only make it easier for us to act on our underlying urge to protect our children by being too involved. And this over-involvement is the problem.

Two cartoons I've kept over the years illustrate parental over-involvement and the issues it causes.

The first cartoon shows three adults: two aging parents with an adult child between them, all sitting in bed together in their pajamas. The dad complains to his wife, "He's forty-seven. He's old enough to cope with nightmares on his own."

In another, a young boy kneels at his bedside saying his evening prayers before going to sleep. His prayer is: "God bless Mom and Dad. Grant them the power to anticipate my every need and the means to fulfill them."

Frazzled Parents

A variant of *Over-Involved Parenting* is the style where the parent's personal anxiety and worry are continually and obviously on display. Conveying ongoing anxiety and insecurity, these parents have a pervasively frazzled demeanor.

The expressed parental anxiety leaves the child with the predominant impression that nobody is minding the store, so to speak.

Take Claudia, a mom of three children ages nine, seven, and five. Claudia tells me that she worries continually about her children throughout her day. Her thoughts swirl around her children's experiences and involvement with school, their friends, and sports and church groups.

This worry exhausts Claudia—and it also diminishes her ability to be decisive. Always afraid to make a wrong move, she conveys a great deal of hesitancy to the children. When she asks her kids to do something, they pick up on this hesitancy and don't do as they are asked. Essentially, they know that her requests can be ignored without repercussions.

Claudia feels overwhelmed by her constant worry over her children, which impacts her sleep and marriage. "My husband and I fight constantly," Claudia says. "He dismisses my worrying, and I think he is being insensitive. It goes on and on."

Detached or Uninvolved Parents

From the hovering style, let's move to the other end of the spectrum and look at the Detached or Uninvolved Style. When it comes to things like screen usage, social functioning or school, these parents do little monitoring of their child.

As a result, these parents don't know much about how their child is spending their time or who they are spending it with. This becomes particularly problematic when the child is in middle school or high school.

Let's look at thirteen-year-old Peter, who recently started eighth grade.

Peter has recently developed a new habit of vaping. As he explains it to me, since his friends all do it too, Peter feels it is "no big deal."

Peter's parents, who do not get along with each other, do not monitor him at all, so they offer no input on his day-to-day functioning.

At school, Peter rarely meets his responsibilities. His teachers believe he has ADD, though they are careful not to say that definitively. Whether Peter has ADD/ADHD or not, his parents' detached style is not helping him.

So, what's the link between Peter's experience of being parented and whatever undesirable thing he's doing? Is the problem that he hasn't gotten enough input from his parents to know what decisions are positive and healthy, hence the vaping and slacking off in school?

Or is he sort of letting himself fail classes on purpose in the hopes of getting more attention, even negative attention, from his parents? Or is it just that he's realized that there is no one watching him, so he can do whatever he wants, and he's not yet mature enough to understand that his decisions will have natural consequences for his academic future and/or his health?

Peter is fundamentally disconnected, with virtually no engagement with anything school-related and no motivation for anything other than playing video games and his developing vaping habit.

While we have seen that parental over-involvement can contribute to a child's bad habits and poor choices, parental under-involvement can do that too, as is the case with Peter.

Authoritarian or Rigid Parents

Though this style is less common nowadays, it does show up on occasion. Rigid or authoritarian parents are demanding and inflexible, highly rule-driven, and tend to use "Because I said so" to an extreme degree.

In contrast to the parents who latch on to a psychological theory as an explanation for their child's difficult behavior, these parents ignore the possibility that their child might be influenced by any psychological variables at all.

For a rigid parent, any neurological difference or even any normal human emotion is no excuse for not complying with parental orders immediately and without question.

Children may obey parents who use this style, but underneath, they often accumulate a great deal of anger and resentment. While the anger is often buried, at least in front of their parents, it often comes out in other ways.

Let's take Ben and Adrienne, who have two boys, ages eleven and eight. Both boys can be challenging, both in school and at home.

Ben believes his wife is too soft and indulgent with the boys, so he adopts a different approach. He does not hit them, but he is always yelling and punishing. Ben's ongoing anger toward the boys becomes difficult for him to contain.

The boys feel that their father is entirely too tough on them, and they struggle to contain their anger. Quietly seething in deep resentment that is clear to me upon meeting them, the boys look for ways to undermine their father.

While they are not overt in expressing their anger and resentment, they may show it in non-compliance. They may also display passive-aggressive behavior (which means they clearly communicate "Fuck you...You can't make me" without directly stating it).

Matter-of-Fact Parents

When I talk to parents about how to shift their parenting styles to help their children, proactive, "matter-of-fact" parenting is generally the style I encourage them to adopt. Here is a brief introduction to this style.

Matter-of-Fact Parents recognize that people (including children) make choices, and these choices have built-in consequences that occur naturally. Depending on the choice the child makes, they may experience positive or negative consequences.

As parents, we are far too often uncomfortable with letting our children experience the natural consequences of their choices, particularly the poor ones. While no one wants a child to make bad decisions, Matter-of-Fact Parents recognize that natural consequences help teach all of us. With each decision (good or bad), a child learns. So, parents who use this style can be hopeful that their child will make better decisions going forward.

This parenting style emphasizes clear communication. Through your language, tone, and attitude, you let your child know where you stand and what you expect of them. There are set boundaries and clear rules. But if your child chooses not to follow the rules, they will need to face the pain that results from their choices.

In my experience, some parents believe that this is already their parenting style: they say they have laid out clear expectations and consequences for their children. However, when I talk with them in more depth, it turns out that they're not using this matter-of-fact model in its fullest sense. Very few people are.

In the next section, we'll talk in more depth about Matter-of-Fact Parenting, but for now, it's time to reflect for a moment.

Summary

There are numerous prevalent parenting styles. It is rare for a parent to be completely one or another. However, certain styles characterize our predominant way of interacting with our children. The styles don't create the issues, but they provide a type of interactive effect.

Taking stock of your style is an important first step as we continue to explore ways of understanding and approaching these children. It may not be easy to determine your style and sometimes looking in the mirror can be hard to do. You may want to have an honest discussion with your spouse or partner or someone else whose opinion you trust. Do the best you can to be non-defensive if you hear something that may be a bit uncomfortable to hear.

Going forward try and keep in mind the concept of a "pie-chart of variables," as this will underlie much of the thinking with the various concepts. The pie-chart will not contain equal pieces, like you would find in a pizza, but will be made up of pieces of various sizes. Some may be large, perhaps one-half of the pie, while others may only be a sliver.

THE ATTITUDE OF PARENTING

A central premise of this book is that the attitude of parenting is the heart of handling challenging children. Once you start practicing the Attitude—the look, sound, and tone of your response to challenging behaviors—your children will start to take notice. You may see them starting to pay slightly more attention to what you are saying, as they understand that you're being particularly clear with them.

This change of attitude typically does not come easily to parents. I like to think of it as a specific and discrete skill. Just like any other skill, this one has to be practiced over time.

As I mentioned in the introduction, this book is not a straightforward how-to book. But the more you reflect on these concepts, take time to practice specific strategies, and take on this new attitude, the more these things will become a part of your everyday parent-child interactions.

You might want to reflect on what you think about your current predominant parenting style and start considering the alternative.

Eventually, a different attitude will become your new normal.

Two Modes of Parenting: Be Strategic, Not Reactive

In this section, we'll dig into the specific style that underlies the Attitude of Parenting.

First, you need to know that we can operate primarily in one of two modes when dealing with a child's challenging behavior: we can be reactive, or we can be strategic.

Reactive Mode: The reactive mode involves little communication, and expectations are not clearly stated beyond perhaps some vague request like, "I need you to be good today." Reactive parenting is typically emotional, heated, and possibly punishment based. Punishments are often not a natural or logical consequence of the child's behavior.

Strategic Mode: If reactive parenting is impulsive, heated, and unclear, then strategic parenting is the opposite. When parents are operating in a strategic mode, they are thinking about the odds that their child will behave in a certain way. As a result, strategic parenting is not nearly as emotional or in the moment.

Of course, you cannot anticipate every situation. Often, because children can make choices pretty suddenly, you need to be nimble and quick on your feet, metaphorically speaking. But even then, thinking strategically will help you.

Parents operating strategically look for the built-in, natural consequences of their child's decisions so they can communicate what those consequences will be. In their stance, attitude and tone, these parents are much more matter-of-fact and objective than parents operating in the reactive mode.

Body Language and Tone

We tend to speak in excited tones when we address a child's issues. But there is a risk that this tone can become too agitated, which can make the child feel defensive and lead us away from legitimate communication.

So, tone and also body language are both quite important, but they are often not discussed enough in parenting books. Examine how you speak and present yourself physically; this will increase the effectiveness of your communication and the likelihood of success. As a general rule, try to speak slower, and speak primarily in first-person ("I" or "we") language.

Ten Rules/Guidelines for Guiding the Attitude of Parenting

To get you started on this shift in attitude, I've compiled ten rules (or we can call them guidelines) to keep in mind as you go forward.

If you "break a rule," don't worry. There will be plenty of opportunity to reset and try again.

#1: Turn Down the Yelling

Over the decades, probably the number one go-to strategy used by parents is yelling.

Yelling is emotional, reactive, and very "of the moment." When you feel angry or irritated, yelling is a natural human reaction, especially when your child has been driving you up the wall.

With challenging kids, we tend to snap at them—and then we yell, and then we yell some more, until, thankfully, either the child falls asleep, or we do.

By the end of this section, I hope you will be equipped with more effective alternatives to yelling.

#2: Turn Down the Talking

Somewhat related to Rule #1 is the fact that we tend to talk (i.e., nag or peck) excessively to our kids. Nagging is a very popular strategy that most parents rely upon, so much so that I jokingly refer to the PNQ or "Parent Nag Quotient."

The thing about nagging is that it usually goes nowhere.

In the old *Peanuts* cartoons with Charlie Brown and friends, parents' voices were represented with a droning "wah, wah, wah" sound. A child listening to their parents telling them what to do would just be hearing "wah, wah, wah" all day long.

This is probably what our children hear when we go on and on with our chattering (nagging). It is no wonder our kids' eyeballs are rolling back in their heads, and no wonder they are tuning us out!

To demonstrate the true impact of talking so much, ask yourself when the last time was that your child agreed with you and said, "You know, you're right. I get it. You're making total sense, and I will change my behavior. Thanks for all of the reminders."

I know the answer already.

In the history of humanity, a child has probably never responded that way to a parent's constant nagging—and the same goes for yelling, too.

#3: Always Think About the Odds

When it comes to specific ways to address challenging child behavior, it's essential to begin continually asking yourself about the odds of a certain behavior occurring.

There's a saying that goes, "The best predictor of future behavior is past behavior."

So, you can learn to connect the dots: Remember how your child has reacted to certain situations in the past, then predict the odds of them reacting similarly in the future.

Let's say the last time you went out for lunch the kids were a challenge and misbehaved. Your son ran around the restaurant disturbing others while your daughter whined continually.

The next time you go to a restaurant, what are the odds they will do something similar? Which outcome would you anticipate—the kids sitting calmly at the table and letting you eat in peace, or the kids being disruptive and difficult?

I think I know where I'd place my bet.

Or let's say that your four-year-old has been very difficult at birthday parties. Typically, he pushes and grabs from other kids. Do you anticipate that he will continue to do these behaviors going forward, or do you think that he will change on his own?

The fact of the matter is that most parents don't really consider the odds—they simply hang on to the hope that their children will be better than the last time. (Look back to the "Hey, Bud" and "Frazzled Parenting" descriptions for some concrete examples of this.)

But when you start thinking realistically about how your child will behave in future situations, it's important to consider the odds in order to begin to make significant and meaningful changes in their behavior.

#4: Use a Front-End Strategy

Once you start to consider the odds of an event occurring, you are on the road to implementing an effective front-end strategy to address the behavior(s) of concern.

The front-end strategy lets the child know very clearly and directly how things are going to go before a situation arises. It helps you make sure that your child understands what you expect of them and what the outcomes of their choices will be.

Here's a small example of a front-end strategy a parent can use with a six-year-old who caused a difficult scene at the last birthday party she attended:

"We need to talk about something. We are going to your cousin's birthday party today. The last time we went to a party you got in a lot of trouble by pushing other children while waiting in line and grabbing their toys. It's not going to go that way today.

"Mommy and Daddy are going to watch you closely. If we see you push or grab or anything like that, we will pull you over and give you one warning. If it keeps up, we will go out to the car and sit there quietly for ten whole minutes. We will then try again. If you continue to misbehave, we go home immediately, and you will have a quiet day at home with no electronics or screens.

"It's totally up to you how the birthday party goes."

This kind of proactive planning puts you firmly in the driver's seat—a place that the parents of challenging children rarely occupy because they often fall into the trap of responding reactively to their child's every behavior.

Again, I want to emphasize that while some of these suggestions may seem obvious, the vast majority of parents who have challenging, difficult children are using a back-end approach, reacting to children in the moment when the behavior occurs.

This is why really internalizing this rule as a parent can be life-changing. Once you combine considering the odds and implementing a front-end strategy, your parenting will become proactive and not reactive—and this will become your new default style.

#5: Have A Few Key Phrases Ready to Go

To help you adopt this proactive, front-end strategy, you need certain key phrases you can say in response to your child's difficult behavior. These phrases allow you to disengage more readily. In other words, they help keep you from "taking the bait" and reacting emotionally.

Over time, as you avoid taking the bait in response to your child's behavior, your child will start to understand that you are no longer so easily manipulated or swayed.

Feel free to make up some of your own, but here are some phrases that I have found to be particularly helpful:

"It's up to you. You decide how you want it to go," can be very powerful. In situations that require your child to make a choice between positive and negative behavior, the phrase effectively lets you sidestep the power struggles that are at the heart of many conflicts.

For example, when children attempt to avoid homework, parents typically try to control the child through pleading, yelling, nagging, or negotiating. But if you shrug and use this "It's up to you" phrasing, you're sending a very different message. You're telling your child that you will let them face the natural consequences, good or bad, of their own behavior.

"Oh, well. I'm sorry you are unhappy." This phrase is best delivered in a calm and direct manner after the child has made a bad choice and the parent has implemented a consequence—like when you send your child to their room right after dinner with no screen time. This phrase lets your child know that you are not willing to rescue them from feeling the discomfort of their choices.

"That's a shame. You'll figure it out." Like the statements above, this phrase powerfully sidesteps power struggles and lets the child know that they are the ones who need to decide.

"Hmm...That's a problem. I'm sorry you're unhappy with the choice you made." This phrase puts the child on notice that you see that the choice they are making will be problematic.

"Could be so." This is a good phrase to use with children who have behavior issues in school and complain that things are so unfair. This phrase neither agrees nor disagrees with your child's statements about unfairness—and that way, you can avoid the vicious cycle of arguing with your child and trying to prove a point.

Fundamentally, these phrases help you to disengage and put the choice on the child, where it belongs. And using this language over time will have a considerable impact on your kid's behavior.

When you use these phrases, just remember that you also need to stick to Rule #4. Your front-end strategy in these situations involves letting your child experience the natural consequences of their own behavior, so make sure you're prepared to follow through on that.

#6: Remember the Child's Primary Motivation

As discussed in the introduction, understanding what children want can bring about a major shift in your thinking. If you embrace this concept, I predict your perceptions will change for the better.

So, what is your child's primary motivation?

At the root of most of their challenging behavior, children are pleasure seekers. They want what they want, when they want it.

This isn't fundamentally different from what *adults* want. We're all pleasure seekers at heart. But the big difference between adults and children is that adults have learned to delay gratification and put pleasure aside, at least theoretically.

Especially if you're a Psychological Theories Parent, you'll notice that as you embrace this principle, you'll lean less heavily on other psychological and/or neurological explanations for your child's behavior.

In other words, you will see things for what they are.

#7: There Are Ways to Express Anger/Displeasure Without Getting Too Hot

We tend to think of anger as a "hot" emotion, and we can hear it in the phrases we use: "boiling mad," "simmering with resentment," "erupting in rage."

Even children who don't seem to care about anything can experience a parent's expression of anger in a powerful and negative way. As noted in Rule #1, anger is usually expressed reactively and forcefully, which can feel quite scary to children.

Sometimes it's appropriate to express anger, but this can be done in more objective and direct tones, without the extra heat.

#8: Look for the Most Natural and Logical Consequence

Parents often deliver punishment as an expression of the anger discussed in Rule #7. This approach tends to be very heavy-handed, and the child typically does not learn anything since they are so enraged by the unfairness of it all. (*This is so stupid,* they think. *I will show them that this won't work.*)

However, if you think through the odds of your child behaving in a certain way and imagine future scenarios, you'll start to see that most situations contain built-in natural consequences.

For instance, when I talk about Rule #5, allowing a child to face the natural consequences of not doing homework, those consequences could be a bad grade in the class, experiencing a sense of failure because some of their friends got better grades, and embarrassment at getting a grade that doesn't reflect their real ability.

These consequences can be delivered as part of your front-end, proactive strategy. Many of the stories that follow this section will illustrate this point.

#9: It's OK to Let Your Child Feel Bad

Somewhere along the way, guilt, or feeling badly about something one has done, has gotten a bad name.

Earlier generations of parents inflicted heavy doses of guilt on their children, often in front of others. As a reaction to this prior generation's approach, parents began to believe that children should not feel bad or guilty about their actions, even egregious actions. Guilt was seen as a psychologically damaging emotion to be avoided at all costs, as children who experienced guilt would become self-doubting and insecure.

In contrast with this view, I think there is some value in letting children feel bad or guilty for doing something wrong. (I can hear the howls of protest as I write this.)

As with other negative feelings like frustration and parental anger, it can be healthy to allow your child to experience guilt, so long as it's done right without adding too much guilt or negativity on top.

There's an old saying that applies here: "Let them stew in their juices." That is, let the person feel bad about what they did. While it may not be popular currently, on some level it may be helpful to allow children to reflect on their actions and feel guilty if that is the natural effect of a bad decision.

If, on the other hand, you do not permit your child to feel the impact of a negative choice, little learning takes place.

#10: Surprise With the Positive

While I emphasize Rule #9 because many parents do not allow their children to feel bad, Rule #10 is important to consider because some parents overemphasize the positive.

This trend largely grew out of the same psychological theories we discussed in relation to guilt and letting children feel bad about things. To counterbalance the predominant feeling that parenting was too focused on the negative, parents and teachers began using lots of positivity, like praise, or tangible rewards, such as smiley face stickers.

To clarify, I certainly don't mean that we should avoid praising or rewarding children—but overdoing the positivity can actually diminish its effectiveness. Praise is a good thing, but if it's constant and indiscriminate, it can simply become more "wah, wah, wah" in the background of your child's life.

You can often hear this overemphasis in parents' language. Many frequently tell their children "You're so amazing!"—when few children's or adults' accomplishments come close to the dictionary definition of that word. Parents are frequently seen cheerleading from the sidelines at sports games or other activities—as in quite literally cheering at every swing of the bat or every shot taken, even when their child strikes out or misses.

This is well-intentioned, since the parents feel they are reinforcing their child's self-esteem. But to the child, all that cheering eventually just sounds like crowd noise.

Relatedly, some parents overuse tangible rewards, like buying their child something for a certain behavior. Of course, there are situations where tangible reinforcement is appropriate, but recognition is often its own reward.

What I tell parents about positive reinforcement is that it's best when it is given in a way that the child does not necessarily expect.

In effect, you "catch them being good" in a way that surprises them. This can be motivating. Kids know that there is something real and authentic about this non-constant praise or reward. They may also think that if they keep up the trend of positive behavior, they might get another surprise reward sometime in the future.

An example of catching them "by surprise," might be something said much later like, "I noticed you were being a good teammate and encouraging to your friend when he struck out. I was very proud of you when you did that." or "I saw you congratulate the other team after the game. That really showed good sportsmanship."

The Proactive-Preventive-Strategic Approach

At the heart of the change of Attitude is what I call "PPSA" ("Proactive-Preventive-Strategic Approach").

The PPSA builds on the rules and principles we've discussed throughout this book. Just like this book focuses on parenting, the parent, not the child, is the target of the approach.

This approach guides parents step by step in dealing with their child's challenging behavior. In fact, I've found that variations of the PPSA can effectively address most behavior issues for most children.

Since logical consequences are a part of the PPSA, parents often think they are already following these recommendations. They will say things like, "We already took away his video game system, and it doesn't seem to make a difference."

However, the PPSA is the opposite of a punishment like taking away a video game system. In my experience, it is rare that a parent truly and fully implements an approach like the PPSA, even if they think they've done so.

Because the PPSA is a proactive approach, like its full name indicates, you start implementing it *before* any event you anticipate may be challenging. Such an event can be just about anything: getting ready for bed, watching TV, going to a restaurant, visiting grandparents, or attending a birthday party.

Step One: Becoming Proactive (Anticipating)

The first step basically involves thinking about the odds that your child will behave in a certain way, as we've been discussing throughout this book.

You know your child's personality and tendencies. And as I've said, the best predictor of future behavior is past behavior. With challenging children, anticipation is particularly important. You need to be more "on your toes" than you would with a child whose temperament is more flexible.

Step Two: Problem Definition and Body Language

Once you have anticipated how your child may act, you can take the next step and define the problem for your child. The key to this step is talking to your child before the event occurs.

Note that tone is essential in this step, since parents tend to speak to their children in overly emotional, rapid, and excitable tones. When this happens, children tune out parents, parents may become reactive, and communication shuts down. Before you talk to your child, practice speaking slowly in a low, objective tone.

Then, define the problem clearly to your child. While you're talking to them, pay attention to your body language. How do you present yourself physically? Try leaning in while you talk. This nonverbally communicates that you mean business and are not being casual. And be sure to pay attention to your child's eye contact during this conversation.

Step Three: Set the Boundaries and Consequences – "Here's What's Going to Happen"

In this step, you set boundaries and establish clear communication. Essentially, you are letting your child know what will happen during the event.

Let's look at a conversation between Stacy, a single parent, and her seven-year-old and five-year-old girls, who are quite challenging for her.

As Stacy explained to me a while ago, the children do not cooperate with her when they go out to eat, and there are almost always moments when one or both children misbehave. This aggravates Stacy and makes it extremely unpleasant for them all to go out. What was supposed to be fun family time becomes the opposite.

Using the PPSA, here's how Stacy now speaks to her children.

She sits them down before they go out. (She thinks proactively and anticipates, as in step one.)

She says, "Girls, we need to talk about something." (She sets the tone and lets them know how it's going to work, and she pays attention to their body language.)

"The last time we went out for pizza, it was very unpleasant. You guys were very uncooperative. There was too much arguing and fighting, and you were not listening to me when I asked you to do certain things. It's not going to be that way when we go out again tonight." (Clearly state in objective language and tone how it will or will not go.)

Statements such as "It's not going to be that way" prove particularly important, as they put you squarely in charge. You let your children know on the front end, proactively, how it will go.

"If you both start behaving the way you did the last time, here's what's going to happen."

Letting the child know "what's going to happen" is an important phrase that signifies there is little ambivalence or "wiggle room." This phrase also helps you to speak in more objective, clear tones.

Stacy continues, "If you start to misbehave and become uncooperative in the car, or when we get to the restaurant, we will turn around and go straight home. No pizza. I will make you a small dinner, and then right after dinner, you will get your pajamas on and go upstairs to your room. There will be no iPads, cell phones, or TV for the rest of the evening. You will be allowed to look at books quietly in bed."

(Wow. You can't get clearer or more objective than that.)

Stacy continues, "If the behavior takes place in the pizza place after we ordered, then as soon as the order comes, we will take it home and you will have your dinner quietly and then get ready for bed. You'll be allowed to look at storybooks quietly in bed until you fall asleep.

"If you are both cooperative, then you can have some time to play on your own before you get ready for bed. That's it. It's your choice how you want this evening to go. It's up to you guys."

Stacy's manner of speaking to her girls is the embodiment of the proactive mode and matter-of-fact style of parenting. She is not hot or reactive. She's clear. There is little room for her kids to misinterpret her, and their possible choices are clear to them.

There is also another proactive phrase you can use: "Here's the deal." For example, Stacy could tell her girls, "Here's the deal. If you cooperate, then you earn screen time when we get home. If you don't, then it's straight upstairs when we get home. It's your choice."

Now, as you and your child move towards the event, whatever it is, there is one last, crucial thing to keep in mind: you must leave the outcome of the event up to your child. As you've just told them, "It's your choice."

Remember that when you adopt this new attitude towards parenting, you can't be invested in the results of your child's choices. You also do not impose your will on them. Power struggles are at the root of so many behavior issues, and in this parenting approach, we simply don't engage in those fights.

It really is your child's choice now. If they choose well, all is right with the world. If they choose poorly, they'll have to live with the negative consequences.

Step Four: "The Event" – How Did It Go?

This is the step where you decide how the event went and whether there will be a positive outcome or negative consequences.

While the child does not have to be perfect throughout the event, they must essentially cooperate within the event for it to be deemed positive. On the other hand, if the child has a hard time and is difficult, then you can consider the outcome negative. This results in the consequences described earlier.

This Approach Differs from Typical Reactive Parenting Modes

Very often, parents in the middle of an event that is not going well are not operating in a proactive mode like the one I've described—they simply react.

The non-reactive PPSA is a big contrast to this. You speak to your kids in a very matter-of-fact tone, and then of course there is the key phrase: "How do you want it to go?" This phrase emphasizes that behavior is a choice. It signals to them that you will not nag or badger them.

So, in many respects, PPSA is the opposite of an emotional reaction.

This statement indicates clearly who is in charge, sets boundaries and establishes clear communication. The parent is direct with the children and lets them know exactly what will happen.

For most parents this does not come quickly or easily. Certain parenting types, such as the pleaser style, will find proactive approaches especially difficult.

In summary, the way you say things, your body language, and your tone are what convey your new parenting attitude to your child. As you speak to them, listen for whether you attempt to use "I" or "we" language or make finger-pointing statements.

You can usually determine this by their response. If your child responds defensively, finger-pointing probably took place. Here's another story to illustrate the process.

Moira's eight-year-old child, Jeremy, has a meltdown because his mother does not respond to all his demands at the supermarket, even though she has already placed a variety of things that he likes in her shopping cart. Jeremy is challenging and makes loud noises to demonstrate his unhappiness.

Practicing PPSA, Moira stays calm and gets on eye level with Jeremy. She lets him know that if he continues his behavior, he will be very unhappy with what will happen. Jeremy ignores his mom, and the demands and meltdowns continue.

In response, Moira calmly turns on her heels and walks back and returns every item in the store. They walk back out to the car, and without yelling or haranguing, Moira drives straight home. All the while, Nicholas cries and whimpers in the back seat. Moira coolly ignores him.

When they arrive home, Jeremy demands his devices. Moira is firm and does not yield to him, even though Nicholas flails on the floor and has a fit and a meltdown.

After a great deal of time passes with Moira completely ignoring Jeremy, the tantrums stop. Moira does not lecture or explain. She goes about her business.

The next day, Moira decides to try grocery shopping again. Before they leave, she says to Jeremy, "Remember what happened yesterday? If that behavior continues, we will turn around and go straight home, like we did yesterday. That was no fun for you, I'm sure. It's up to you how you want it to go. It's one way or the other."

Aaron and Blake: Raging, Cursing Brothers

We know that siblings fight. This goes back to biblical times.

However, Aaron and Blake, ages thirteen and eleven, hold the house hostage with their constant arguing, which often becomes physical. They scream things like, "You're a fucking asshole" or "Fuck you, you dick."

Their parents feel completely overwhelmed by the fighting and the cursing, as if the household is being terrorized and they are being held hostage.

Here's a conversation that Francine, their mom, might have with her sons as she practices the Attitude of Parenting:

"Guys, we need to talk. Dad and I are extremely upset with what has happened around the house. There is entirely too much fighting, and the cursing is out of control. This is going to stop. Here's the deal. If you guys fight like you did yesterday, there will be serious consequences."

For most modern boys, the prospect of losing their phones, iPads, or gaming system is effective, so Francine makes this the natural consequence of poor choices. She says, "If you choose to fight, then for the three to four hours afterwards, there will be zero screen usage and no playing outside. It's up to you how you want it to go."

The key is that when Francine does eventually deliver this consequence, she does not frame it as a punishment.

As I mentioned earlier, many parents think they are using the PPSA or something like it when they take away a game system or phone.

But the difference is that when device removal is delivered as a punishment, the parent is invested in the result, and their tone, delivery, and language are reactive. "You'd better stop the fighting, or else no iPads for the rest of the evening. That's it—give them to me now!" the parent might shout.

But since Francine is making device removal a natural consequence, she is not invested in the result of her sons' decision. It's their choice how it will go. The boys choose to continue fighting, and when Francine tells them to hand over the iPads, her tone conveys the message: "Oh well, I guess you chose poorly. Maybe tomorrow you will figure it out."

By speaking in objective tones, Francine is letting the boys know that they will not hold her hostage or terrorize the household. At the end of the specified three or four hours, she will say something to them like, "Are you ready to try again?"

Responding Effectively by Using a Saying or a Mantra

Dealing with a child's challenging behavior during an event can be incredibly stressful. Many parents find that adopting a mantra, which is a simple, short phrase that you repeat to yourself, helps them to keep a cool head and respond effectively.

Here's a mantra that works for many people—in fact, this is one I use when family relations become strained. I say to myself, *"Don't take the bait."*

Let's take young Mason, a very bright boy I evaluated and worked with along with his parents. Mason was giving his mother fits with his ongoing "shenanigans." His mom, Amy, described an event where she recently took Mason and his brother, along with a couple of friends, to a "bouncy place" where kids could jump on bouncing balls and trampolines.

Amy had booked the bouncy place for about an hour and a half. Characteristic of Mason, after about ten minutes, he started to whine and complain that he was bored and wanted to go home.

Naturally, Amy became quite upset, explaining to him that she paid a lot of money to give him and his friends a fun time. Mason argued back, explaining why he thought it was boring and not fun. Amy kept countering his argument, but eventually, he wore his mom down. They ended up leaving early, with Amy very upset about the whole experience.

Some weeks later Amy and her family were going on a vacation to a beautiful resort. Before the trip, she and Mason came to see me, and she explained that she was dreading the vacation because she feared that Mason was going to complain constantly. Mason would only want to play his video games, she said, and it would ruin the family vacation.

I said to Amy, "We're going to take care of that, and you will have a great time. You need to practice this mantra that you can repeat to yourself over and over: 'Don't take the bait... Don't take the bait.'"

I then explained to Amy (and Mason) that it was okay if Mason chose to be miserable. "That's up to him, and you can't change that," I said to her. "Mason has two choices: to enjoy and take part in the family vacation or to be miserable sitting in a chair—without access to iPads iPhones, or anything like that. It's up to him."

I asked Mason what he thought, and I teased him, telling him that he should say, "Yes, you are brilliant and wise, Dr. Selznick." Mason laughed when I said that, and I knew that I had him, because he knew I was 100% right.

Based on his mom's surprised reaction, I could see that this possibility was a revelation for her. She could let him be miserable if he chose to, and by using the "Don't take the bait" mantra, she could opt out of the whole cycle of whining and arguing.

When the parents came back from the resort, Amy sent me a glowing email saying what a wonderful time they had. I joked with her that the next time they go, they have to take me too!

When the child manages things well, praise them and put a nice check on a visible calendar—a paper one, not on your phone.

That's it.

Usually, in these situations, parents expend all kinds of energy, yelling, arguing, cajoling, and getting themselves all worked up. It's exhausting and depleting. But a parent operating in a proactive mode simply shrugs and says "oh, well," which requires little to no effort. It puts the choice squarely where it belongs—on the child. When you do not give fuel to a fire, it dies out over time.

You can also explain your parenting approach to your child during moments of openness, such as "tuck in time."

Summary

This section drills down on the essence of the attitude. This essence is tied into the phrase "be strategic – not reactive." With this mindset you will turn the heat down and start implementing a different attitude. When you are feeling stressed by how your child is coping (or not coping as will likely be the case), the Attitude will be like a "go-to" strategy you can pull out.

PPSA is a structure, a model that can be applied to most child situations. The model is a step-by-step approach that can be easily followed. The ultimate goal is to put the choice squarely on the child (where it belongs) so that the child is in a position to make decisions.

By giving the child a choice, power struggles are immediately side-stepped, if not eliminated. This process can be started early in the child's life and continued through to college. (OK, in theory at 18 they are adults, anyway and should be starting to make their own decisions.)

Adults are reluctant to have natural consequences, especially unpleasant ones, yet these will provide teachable moments that will have considerable impact and probably be long lasting.

Different from applying punishments which are usually delivered in the heat of the moment, these result in the child having to reflect on the choices made with the hope that better ones will be made going further.

SIGNS OF SUCCESS

First Look to Yourself

One of the first measures of success when it comes to implementing the attitude concepts is surprisingly not centered on your child, but on you as the parent.

Commonly parents rely on two "go-to" strategies when it comes to handling child behavior issues – yelling and/or punishment (usually in the form of a time-out).

Both of these strategies are typically administered in the heat of the moment and are quite reactive.

With the attitude concepts you will see a noticeable shift in yourself (recognizing that things are never completely 100% one way or another).

Some of the Signs

It has been previously mentioned that tone, body language and word choice (phrasing) are important. As you come to practice the concepts (and it does take practice to break long ingrained habits) you may see some of the following.

- Many fewer words will be spoken when it comes to what you are looking for with your child. That is, there will be an efficiency in the way you speak that tends to "cut to the quick" rather than the usual verbal harangue that comes when a child has crossed the line.

- You may find yourself using certain phrases that were not commonly uttered by you in the way you speak to your child. For example, going to a cousin's birthday party (the last one was disastrous), you might say something in the car very clearly like, "Here's the deal…" and then proceed to explain (very briefly) what will occur if things get out of hand.

There will be a greater emphasis to speak slower and clearer while making good eye contact with the child. You will be watching for signs that your child has followed you and understood. There will be no ambiguity in what you are saying. To make 100% sure the child has understood, you may be asking things like, "Now play back what you heard me say," to make sure it has fully registered.

- Another language change that you may notice will be the increased use of the first person, as in "I need you to pick up your clothes," again delivered with little ambiguity, hesitancy, or insecurity in the way the request is made.

- Another key phrase, which may be the distilled essence of the entire Attitude is the statement to the child that, "You have a choice. It's up to you how you want it to go."

This is powerful because it removes the ongoing power struggles that typically take place. When you really mean it and can let the child make good and bad choices, this has enormous implications.

When I asked a parent who reported great success (after I met their six-year-old child one or two times), the parent stated:

"The approach of turning our conversation into a "choice" was very successful. We adapted our language from a behavior-repercussion framework to putting out the choices in front of Noah and then putting the ball in his court. I think this gave him a feeling of control that made him much easier to deal with and behave better."

Bear in mind that with these parents and their very challenging six-year-old there were no behavioral charts or rewards used. The consequences were built into the choices that were made by Noah.

- You will notice yourself thinking more like a gambler. In other words, you will be asking yourself the fundamental question, "What are the odds?" in any given situation, recognizing the best predictor of future behavior is past behavior. So, if the child misbehaved the last time you went to a restaurant, the odds are pretty good that misbehavior will occur again.

- There will be a greater emphasis on vigilance and the child will know you're keeping your eye on things. While you can let your guard down and have a nice time at the backyard barbecue with friends, relatives, and an easier temperament child, the child of concern will have you always keeping one eye out (as much as possible). Knowing the odds and thinking like a gambler reminds you to be vigilant. It also sends a clear message out to the child (again with very few words).

- Rather than create consequences, there will be a recognition that most choices have built-in natural consequences. While we as parents may not like the consequence (e.g., failing a class for not handing in work), the built-in consequences usually have a great deal of power, more so than a made up one like "Time Out" or frowny face on a sticker chart would.

- There is no age range that these changes are specifically geared for. The earlier you let the child experience the impact of their choices (good or bad), the better down the road when the stakes really change as teenagers. The phrase, "Oh well, you made your choice" will have far reaching impact.

- As a parent you will be less concerned about letting your child feel bad if they have made a poor choice. Even if the child has been shown by some practitioners to have ADHD, these concepts still apply.

- Repeating the mantra, "Don't take the bait" will get you out of a variety of challenging moments with your child who is constantly baiting the hook to try and get what it is they want (pleasure and immediate gratification). By not taking the bait, you will be going about your business even if the child is having a meltdown.

Changes in Children

The biggest change in children of the challenging variety will be the recognition over time that someone (you) is minding the store more effectively. With the seed planted that they are in charge of themselves and that with freedom of choice comes consequence, this starts to work into their psyche.

Such children will start to see things like access to a phone or an iPad as a built-in right, rather than a privilege. Since it is a privilege, it can be revoked, like a teenager's access to a car. Keys are given, and keys can be taken away. It's as simple as that.

If the child wants to drive a car, then there are important parameters to follow. It's no different with screen usage. If the screens are abused and the cooperation is minimal, "Oh, well, that's too bad, but for now you've lost the privilege." That's not a punishment; it's a natural consequence.

Here are a few brief examples of changes that kids show after realizing their parents have changed their manner of approaching them:

Lucas

Let's take a look at Lucas, a 16-year-old who is frequently in conflict with his parents. As the parents tell me examples of what they perceive to be Lucas's self-centeredness, what strikes me is how willing they are to be servile to his moods and whims.

A recent example should highlight this and how we focused on a shift in their attitude to look to correct the problem. According to the dad, Lucas would frequently be dropped over at his girlfriend's house in the evening and told that his father would later pick him up at 11:00.

Lucas's father, Bill, arrives at 10:55 and texts Lucas that he has arrived. Ten minutes goes by and there is no response. After 20 minutes Bill tries to call him, but there is no answer.

Since it is so late, Bill doesn't want to knock on the door. As Bill told me the story, he stated, "Well, I really didn't mind. I'm happy to catch up on reading some things on my phone."

At 11:35 Lucas saunters out and gets in the car saying nothing.

As Bill tells me the story, I can feel my blood pressure rising as I want to jump out of my skin and shake William up to help him understand how servile he has become to Lucas. Effectively, Bill is so used to it with Lucas that behaviors such as this go largely unnoticed.

As we talk about it further, Bill starts to understand, and he begins to see how much he's been taken advantage of his good nature.

Coaching Bill on using a PPSA mindset, he later has a sit-down with Lucas. Without turning up the heat, he informs

Lucas clearly that he will be getting there just before 11. He tells Lucas, "Here's the deal. I will give you five minutes leeway, but if it goes beyond that and I'm waiting for you, then the privilege of going to your girlfriend's house is revoked. It's completely your choice—I won't be upset if you choose poorly, but I am not going to make it nice for you either. Your call."

The next time Lucas was taken to his girlfriend's house, without any reminder or cajoling, he walked out at 11:03.

Case closed.

Zion

Zion is an 8-year-old whirlwind. When not getting his demands met in the way he wants, Zion screams at his parents and tells them he hates them and that they are stupid. Even at eight, his screaming is often laced with cursing at them.

One of the ongoing problems is that the dad has been the personification of the "Hey Bud – Parent as Best Friend" style. This has caused considerable tension between the parents, as the mom feels she is constantly undermined.

As noted by the mom, Dad is "definitely the buddy or the fun one. This puts a lot of stress on me as the mom. It's been a work in progress, but Dad has been working on finding the fine line between disciplinarian and fun guy. We find that Zion doesn't like it when Dad acts as the authoritative figure and often he talks back or argues with him.

"We're working on consistency and there is still work to do, but we feel progress is being made. When we team up as parents and support each other, we notice Zion is more responsive."

My answer to the mom was, "Try and remember that we're not interested in whether Zion likes it or not. If he chooses well, good things will come. If not, then so be it." Some may find such a statement unnecessarily harsh, but by all reports Zion (and buddy Dad) are finding an acceptable zone in the household.

Sophia

Sophia is a spunky and artistic 9-year-old. She loves drawing, decorating, and making designs on her iPad.

Sophia also enjoys ignoring her parents.

Sophia is starting to alienate other kids in school too, as she always thinks if her hand shoots up first, then the teacher should be calling on her; she gets upset when others are called before her. She has a hard time picking up on social cues and she perceives others are just mean to her.

How can Sophia be helped? How can the parents be helped?

Like the parents mentioned above, they, too, have been catering to her needs, wants, and demands. This has placed her front and center to a fault.

In a session with Sophia and her parents, we have an open discussion about how Sophia's choices are not serving her well. Sophia's parents strengthen their resolve, and they discuss a few built-in consequences (both of the negative and positive varieties).

A contract between Sophia and her parents is drawn up with goals established as to how things are going to be with her. Sophia happily signs the contract and seems to clearly understand what is being expected.

When Sophia returns a few weeks later she is quite proud of herself and explains how well she did, which was confirmed by her parents. Sophia draws a colorful picture of how she lived up to her end of the contract.

She walked out happily with a few extra stickers of her choosing, looking forward to earning more the next time.

Questions & Answers

Will these children become more flexible of temperament?

The old expression of "leopards not changing their spots" applies here. Temperament is temperament, and I would not be looking for the child to have major transformations. I would be looking for greater flexibility and choices that tend to be more positive in nature.

What about rewards?

I'm not big on rewards, preferring to look for the built-in consequence (positive or negative). The reward of not driving recklessly is that you continue to be able to use the car. The reward of getting off your iPad when it's time to get ready for bed is the reward of being able to use the iPad the next day.

With that said, especially with young children, I am a fan of getting a chart and keeping simple track of mostly positive and cooperative days with a fun sticker. After about 10 stickers or so, surprise them with a "How about we go get an ice cream treat together in recognition of how cooperative you've been?" Everyone likes a good ice cream treat and it's not going over the top on the reward side of things.

All the professionals I know are big on "time out." Why don't you use it?

Time out has its place, but I think it's overused. Often, the child is sent to their room during "time out". They typically have some device up there and being in the room represents a form of escape from parents who are getting on the child's nerves.

You seem to downplay the age of the child as a factor. Why is that?

To my way of thinking, whether the child is 6 or 16, they want their proverbial bread buttered on both sides. While that may sound cynical to some, I think of it as the nature of childhood. Maturity represents being able to put aside your immediate needs and desires to do something you may not want to do, like getting ready for work, taking out the trash, preparing for the next day, etc. These tasks may not be fun, but they need to be done. A mature person understands that. A child is, by definition, a non-mature person. This is especially so with the Group B (challenging) children.

What about therapy for children? You don't seem to mention it?

The approach we take with an individual child depends on the nature of the issue we're addressing. Earlier in my career, I did a lot of individual counseling or therapy with children that involved various forms of play to help the child. For the issues we've been discussing, I like to have the child and one or both parents present to discuss how things are being managed. I try and get each person to tell their view of what took place at, say, the birthday party or a during bedtime issue. Having everyone together helps family members listen to and better understand each other.

What about homework cooperation or lack of it?

Presuming the homework is within the child's legitimate capability, ask yourself what the natural outcome of not cooperating during homework time is. The answer is simple: "You don't give, you don't get." For most modern children their driving passion is screen usage. Just shrug and tell the child that the privilege has been revoked for the night, with no yelling, haranguing, or lecturing. My money would be on greater cooperation the next night.

What if my child has been found by the pediatrician to have ADHD? What then?

This question is challenging because underneath it is the belief that because of ADHD, the child is neurologically unable to behave more flexibly or cooperatively.

A few points to consider:
- There is no test or x-ray that says objectively whether a child does or does not have ADHD.
- Typical diagnoses are offered after a review of the child's history and a questionnaire which has been filled out

by the parents. The questionnaire, by its nature, is subjective.

- Even if we fully go along with the notion that the child has a neurobiological disorder, my perspective would be that it is even more reason to implement the strategies suggested in this book.

- Children with ADHD, perhaps even more so than typical kids, need to know parameters and limits. Structure is enormously important to them. It's my opinion that changing how you behave as a parent helps to set the structure better for them, so they know how things will work in most situations.

What about medication? Are you pro or con?

Really, I'm neither completely for nor completely against medication. I've seen some kids who have been helped by going on medication and many who have not. It's important to remember that the primary purpose (as I understand it) of ADHD medication is to help the child focus more effectively. One can be better focused and still have meltdowns when they're not getting what they want.

Do you think things are different now than they were a generation or two ago?

As I mentioned earlier in the text, for thousands of years, parents have been shaking their collective head about unruly children. With that said, I do think today's parents are grappling with a new and different issue as children and teens are becoming increasingly screen addicted. Many of the kids I see seem to care about nothing else but getting back on their screens and I find this very concerning. Whether this is a generational problem or not, I really have no idea, but my gut is telling me that we are not adequately addressing the underlying issues or truly understanding the long-term effects.

Final Thoughts:
"This, too, shall pass"

Let's go back to one of the early fundamental truisms: "Challenging children are challenging."

There will be a variety of different opinions and perspectives on what is needed for these children.

The perspective here is that parents are not the cause of challenging behavior in their children. Instead, it's the combination of and interaction between parenting styles and the child's natural tendencies that can create a toxic brew.

The central premise here is that children are largely in one camp or another, based on their temperament: Those who are flexible and those who are demanding and more challenging.

Parents are presented as the agents of change. It is felt that in increments with a different mindset, a different attitude can begin to turn things around and change the odds.

Parenting has its own built-in challenges whether the child is of the easier and more flexible or of those that are challenging and difficult.

I have known many kids throughout much of their young lives, having tracked them from early childhood through their high school years and beyond.

Parents will often contact me some time after I have lost touch with the family. They will frequently report that the challenging years are mostly behind them and their child, now a legitimate adult, has grown up—and they have too.

When they tell me these stories, I feel a sense of gratitude for having been a part of the formative years and the challenges that the family faced and addressed together.

Time and again, I return to the wisdom that helps many parents have perspective while taking the long view – "This, too, shall pass."

Influences & Resources

My most significant influence has been the reactions of parents and children to my work with them. Of course, I'm sure I've made some misses along the way, but I'd like to believe I've also had a number of hits and these successes have given me the fuel to present these concepts to you. Every professional who works with children and families is shaped by many factors, including their schooling, training, philosophy, continuing education, the books they've read, and other influences too numerous to name. All of these factors combine to shape a professional's perspective on how best to help children and families, just as they have for me. I encourage you to read further and utilize the resources below.

- One book that impacted my thinking and approach is *The Difficult Child,* by Ross Greene with its emphasis on temperament as a ruling variable in child behavior. (www.drrossgreene.com)
- When my children were young, there was a parenting column that I read frequently called, *On Parenting,* by John Rosemond. The column always aways made sense to me in terms of his advocating a no-nonsense approach

with children while disavowing certain popular trends in parenting. A number of his books are on my shelf – I would recommend, *Because I Said So* as an introduction (www.rosemond.com).

- A longtime "Parent Guru" that I have enjoyed is Dr. Michele Borba. I am honored to have Michele's endorsement for "Beyond the Power Struggle." Check out her website and books. She is a great resource. (www.micheleborba.com)
- *Parenting With Love & Logic* also has stayed firmly in my psyche over the years as an influence and touchstone. Check them out: (www.loveandlogic.com)
- Dr. Sarah Allen has wonderful books and a great website (https://www.brainbehaviorbridge.com). Her support of *Beyond the Power Struggle* is greatly appreciated.

About the Author

Dr. Richard Selznick is a psychologist, nationally certified school
psychologist, assistant professor
of pediatrics, school consultant,
Wilson Certified Dyslexia in-
structor, and Certified Dyslexia
Advocate. As the Director of the
Cooper Learning Center, a di-

vision of the Department of Psychiatry at Cooper University
Healthcare, he oversees a program that assesses and treats a
broad range of learning and school-based behavioral problems
in children.

Dr. Selznick has presented to parents and educators inter-
nationally, as far as Dubai and Abu Dhabi and throughout the
United States. A down-to-earth speaker who presents complex issues in non-jargon terms, he has a particular passion for
helping parents understand dyslexia and related reading disorders. He facilitates parenting groups and is called upon by local
community groups to offer his understanding of parenting and

raising children in the 21st century. *Beyond the Power Struggle: A Guide for Parents of Challenging Kids* is his sixth book.

To learn more about Dr. Selznick, and to receive his blog, go to www.shutdownlearner.com. You can follow him on "X" (formerly Twitter) (@DrSelz); Instagram (@shutdown_learner); YouTube (subscribe to "Dr. Richard Selznick") and on Facebook under The Shut-Down Learner.

Dr. Selznick is available for online chats on parenting challenging behavior, dyslexia, learning disabilities and related topics. Email rselz615@gmail.com for more information.

Acknowledgements

I want to express my heartfelt gratitude to all the families who have entrusted me to work with their children, each while facing unique struggles in different areas of their lives. Both the parents and the children have taught me so much along the way.

Many thanks as well to Cooper University Health System for their ongoing support, not only for me but also for the Cooper Learning Center. I believe there are very few large health systems in the country that have a program like ours dedicated to the assessment and intervention of reading problems, and for that, I am deeply grateful. Thanks as well to all the staff at the Cooper Learning Center. Your devotion to the children and the mission of the program goes above and beyond.

As always, thanks to my editor, Stephanie Manuzak, for keeping me motivated and helping to bring this book to life.

Finally, I would like to take this opportunity to thank my wife Gail and my family and friends for their ongoing support and encouragement. There were times when I started to feel my motivation waning during this project, and they consistently helped me to reset and recharge.